Table of Contents

Chapter 1 – No Contraception and No Money

On June 26th 1957, in the small town of Warrington, England, a midwife visited the home of Hazel and Douglas Donlan to perform a home delivery of their seventh and final child, yours truly. My mother confided in me when I was older that she had planned to have only four children, and not seven. She said she had always considered the perfect size family to be two parents with four children. I concluded from this that it was undoubtedly a thrilling experience for my mother when she found she was pregnant for the fifth, sixth and seventh times! My parents were was not in any way, shape or form religious people but they clearly adhered to the teachings of the Bible, "Be fruitful and multiply."

I do not recall much of my early childhood, just some odds and ends here and there. When I was about eleven years old, we moved to a new home on Algernon Street in Warrington. Our new home was situated at the end of a row of houses. It had been a grocery store at one time and across the middle of the front window the word, "Cadbury's" was printed in frosted glass in large words. My parents had bought this house with the intention of opening it up as an electrical business. After my parents had moved into the house they were disappointed because they were informed that the area was now zoned for residential purposes only and this meant that their new house could not be opened as a business. My father decided to go into business with a friend of his and they opened an electrical business in a store located fairly close to our home on Lovely Lane in Warrington. It is my understanding that my father became disgruntled with his partner because he did not fulfill many of his work responsibilities. They unfortunately closed the business and separated from each other under bitter circumstances.

My mother told me she became tired of having no money because Dad's income from his electrical work was insufficient. She decided to take things into her own hands and went to nursing school to become a nurse and then she went on further to become a midwife. According to my mother, my father was an excellent writer but he lacked the self confidence he needed to return to school. My mother acknowledges she should have encouraged education more in our home, but back in those days she says, and in the area in which we lived, education was not emphasized. My two sisters and I each learned the basics pretty well in school, but my four brothers were not as fortunate. I remember my brother Stephen's school report card stated, "Daydreams" and the following year his report card stated, "Still daydreams!" Today we call this attention deficit disorder and in retrospect this is probably what he had!

I do not think my brothers' situation is unusual because I expect many individuals find themselves in a similar position. I suspect that in many instances the main difference between an individual in the academic field and an individual in the blue collar field is that the person in the blue collar field may simply not have had an opportunity placed on academics or they may be intimidated and lack the confidence to attend college. I have witnessed this with my own brother, Kevin. He literally broke out into a sweat when I took him to visit my college campus a few years ago. I was shocked at how intimidated and insecure he was on the college grounds and yet he excels in any employed position he holds and receives awards for being an exemplary employee.

When I was much younger and attended school in England, I was not a serious student. I remember skipping school frequently with my friend, Angela. On one of the typical days when we were skipping school and walking along the street, we were actually stopped by a truant officer. She must have thought Angela and I looked suspicious because she stopped us to ask why we were not in school. Fortunately, I had anticipated this potential event and I was prepared with the appropriate answers to her questions to hide the fact that we were actually skipping school. Questions the truant officer asked included which school Angela and I attended and what grade level we were in. I answered the truant officer being careful to give 'the right' answers that matched the ones she had in her notes. She asked, "Which subject do you currently have?" To which I replied, "Community service." She checked her list and confirmed that this

4

answer fits appropriately with the class periods at our school. She smiled warmly and told us to keep up the good work, and then she sent us on our merry way! I had the name and address of an elderly person available to give to the truant officer, just in case she had wanted to confirm our information further. This elderly person really did exist and she knew me quite well, and so I expected she would have unwittingly collaborated our story if the truant officer had taken us to her house to confirm our information. Angela and I both agreed after this event that it had been too close for comfort. We were both anxious during the time the truant officer was speaking to us, and we knew we would have been in serious trouble if she had realized we really were guilty of skipping school!

I began to actively choose to do non-traditional female activities after we moved to Algernon Street when I was about twelve years old. I became indignant and I subsequently behaved in a quietly rebellious manner when I realized because I am female there is an expectation I will naturally enjoy feminine activities such as cosmetics and painting nails. In reality, I considered these activities to be a total waste of my time and I had no interest in participating in them. I became quite a tomboy and I realized I was attracted to activities that boys typically enjoy. My first male friend was Gary McAndrews, a dark haired and handsome eleven year old boy. I initially met Gary at our local park. His nickname was 'Mouse' because he had a squeaky voice. Mouse and I became instant friends and he introduced me to his friends which included his younger brother, Tommy. We hung out together from thereon in our plentiful free time. We climbed trees and built extravagant camps out of wood others had thrown out. I was the only girl in this group of friends but I didn't care and I was appreciative that the boys allowed me to hang out with them. At an earlier time I had concluded that boys do more exciting activities together and they have more fun compared to girls. However, there was a price I had to pay for being the only girl in the group. For example, Mouse and the boys loved to take my shoes and throw them up into a tree. Being the proud soul that I was, I would climb the trees myself in bare feet to retrieve my shoes. Unfortunately however, there was one tree that nobody but Mouse could climb. If my shoe was thrown up into this particular tree, I was dependent on Mouse to return the shoe to me. I was not at all satisfied to be dependent on Mouse in this way and so I decided to take care of this problem once and for all. One day, I purposefully stayed behind while Mouse and his friends left to enjoy a fun day at one of our favorite places to hang out, the Dingle Forest. I, instead, spent that particular day at the park, and I practiced for hours, learning to climb the dreaded tree that only Mouse could climb. There were no limbs on the tree to serve as foot supports and the tree had such smooth bark that my feet slid down the tree as I attempted to climb, over and over again. I was determined to climb this tree and I was exhausted with sore, bloody feet, but by the end of the day I had eventually mastered the task. I was eager to show off my new accomplishment the next time Mouse threw my shoe up into 'his' tree. The boys all watched in amazement as I smiled confidently and began to climb 'Mouse's tree'. I gripped the tree tightly with my arms and legs and then climbed the tree with bare feet. I was thrilled to display my accomplishment and grab my shoes from the branches and then I slid back down the tree. Mouse was noticeably disappointed to realize I was no longer at his mercy to retrieve my shoes and this event served to mark the end of the shoe tree throwing activity!

Chapter 2 – Pre-teen Years

Our group had a special loud, high pitched call that we used to communicate with each other when group members were at opposite ends of the park, to indicate we wanted to get together. I was not impressed with our call because anybody could mimic it. My father could wolf whistle really well and I was able to master a similar technique by copying him. However, he would use his thumb and index finger from the same hand and blow hard with them placed, finger tip to finger tip, to form a circle with his fingers, pushed up against the underside of his curled up tongue. My whistle technique is to place the tips of my straight index and middle fingers from each hand, pushed up against the underside of my curled up tongue, to form the base of a 'v' shape against my tongue, and then I blow hard through the middle of these fingers to produce a very loud, shrill, high pitched whistle. My dad and I could whistle very loud and I practiced my new found, shrill and loud whistle outside our house. My parents told me to stop practicing my whistle technique because the neighbors complained to them about the noise. I had not realized my neighbors would not appreciate my new found skill as much as I did!

I was happy to demonstrate my new whistle technique to my friends, and I suggested this whistle would be more suitable to use as our group call rather than the high pitched voice call. I told the boys the voice call wasn't loud enough to be our communication signal. The boys all agreed and so I taught each of them how to wolf whistle. This then became our official call and we were satisfied with our new and improved more respectable method of communication.

I was the only group member who had never fallen and broken a bone and I wanted it to remain that way. I suspect the reason for this is that girls are naturally more cautious than boys. One of our favorite places to hang out was on a small uninhabited island, which we named Monkey Island. On this island, we would actually grab onto a rope which hung from a tree in order to swing out over the

River Mersey. At the time, this river had a fluffy, white, undoubtedly toxic chemical on its surface. The river reminded me of a huge meringue! It must have been a sight for anybody to see in broad daylight, six preteens, hanging onto a rope which was swinging over the River Mersey! I remember one unfortunate day; the police arrived and scolded us for playing on the island. They told us our activities were dangerous and they insisted we leave. We never set foot on Monkey Island again but the fun memories are forever present!

We soon found another fun activity. We would hang out in some old vacant houses which were scheduled to be demolished. Unfortunately, once again, the police arrived and put an end to this play time as well. We had heard police sirens and, suspecting the worst, we all ran to hide, just in case we were not supposed to be playing in the abandoned houses. Mouse and the others all ran to hide under the stairs. I instead went my own way and hid in a small cupboard that housed a gas meter. I was surprised because the police actually had dogs with them, and unfortunately for the boys, they were instantly sniffed out by the dogs in their hiding place under the stairs. I was more fortunate because the odor from the gas meter camouflaged my presence in the small cupboard and the dogs could not pick up my scent. But my luck ran dry as I heard a grumpy sounding, elderly man, who had apparently tipped off the police about our presence in the houses, insisting to the police that there were two redheads. He, in fact, was correct, because Johnny Gallop and I both had red hair. I was relieved and impressed to hear Johnny tell the police and the grumpy old man that it only appeared two redheads were present because he had been standing in front of a mirror. This explanation was accepted as legitimate and so the police ended their search for an additional red head! Each of the boys was taken home by the police and grounded for several days. I was very grateful to Johnny for coming to my defense. He would have been in serious trouble if the police had discovered me because they would have realized Johnny had lied. Johnny's lie to police was very much out of character for him and I remember being taken aback and grateful as I heard him come to my defense.

I stayed crouched in the gas meter cupboard for several hours because I was too cautious to come out any sooner. During this time, the grumpy old man returned and I heard him speaking to another person. He said, "We can go in and get the carpet now because the coast is clear!" It became apparent to me that this man had reported us to the police because he wanted to claim some items from the empty houses for himself. These were items which had been left purposely by the former residents of the abandoned houses because they no longer had need for them. Obviously, the grumpy old man considered the items to be of value to him and he made sure some pesky teens did not interfere with his acquisition of them. As soon as I was able to leave without being seen, I climbed out of the window and ran home. I felt quite sore and stiff because I had spent several hours crouched in the tiny cupboard with no space to stretch. Still, I knew my fortune was preferable to my friends' outcome because I was not grounded for several days, and for that I owed Johnny Gallop a big thank you!

Yet another time the police became involved in our extracurricular activities was when we challenged another group of teens to a game of tug-of-war on our park's immaculately manicured bowling green. I had stepped off the bowling green to take a break from the game and I noticed a police car parked on the road alongside the park. I thought it would be fun to pretend the police had arrived to round us up and so I yelled to the other teens, "Police! Run!!" It did not occur to me that the police really had arrived to round us up! We were totally unaware of the damage we were causing as we dug the heels of our shoes into the beautifully manicured velvet green grass of the bowling green. We never considered that somebody might be upset about our activities on the lawn and report us to the police. After I had yelled out to everyone, I was laughing because of my joke on everybody, and I ran aimlessly with my eyes closed because everybody scattered in a hysterical panic. I was still unaware the police really were present to catch each of us and take us home to our parents for appropriate punishment. As I continued to run gleefully with my eyes still closed, I suddenly slammed into a large, tall solid structure. I gingerly looked up and realized I had collided with an enormous, surly-looking, policeman. He did not thaw in the least despite my nervous smile, and I apologized profusely for running into him. He looked down at my skinny, timid structure and he spoke sternly to me. He pointed to a park bench and then growled, "You sit there!" I obediently sat down on the bench and he left me to sit alone while he proceeded to round up the others. I stayed put on the bench as he had ordered and I expected he would be back to get me and take me home for my sentencing. But he did not return. All was now quiet and dark. I watched a police car drive up and down the park field, shining a large flashlight, looking for any remaining rascals. As the police car drove down over the hill and out of sight, I seized the moment to make a quick escape across the field, in the hopes of not being seen. I made it across the field successfully and I then scrambled up and over the park wall to my freedom, outside of the park. I caught my breath on the other side of the wall and I then walked, as inconspicuously as possible, along the side street and I turned to walk on the street of the main road. I was surprised to see Mouse walking toward me. We grinned and congratulated each other for having such wonderful survival skills and for escaping capture from the police. Within seconds however, a police car drove up from behind us and a policeman inside the car wound down his car window, growled and ordered, "Get in!" The policeman took us home and he spoke briefly to my father. I was reprimanded by my father after the policeman left and I was sent me up to my room.

On a day shortly thereafter, I was sent to my bedroom for some minor misdeed and I remember being upset that I was being treated unfairly. I therefore rebelled and foolishly decided to climb out through my bedroom window and over the corrugated garage roof, hoping not to crack it due to my burdensome weight of a whole 99 pounds! I climbed down the wall, gripping onto the drain-pipe with my hands while my feet were pressed up against the wall. I ran to Saint Elphin's park and joined my friends to kick a soccer ball around for about two hours. I didn't pay much attention to the time and I left the park and ran home around dinner time. I climbed back up the drain-pipe and tread quietly and carefully back over the corrugated garage roof. Just as I climbed in through the bedroom window my mother called up the stairs to me, "Okay Denise, you have been in there long enough, you can come out of your room now!" I was obviously fortunate in this case that I was not caught misbehaving. I certainly was blatant in my behavior; so blatant that I really should have been caught in my act of defiance. It was sheer luck that I made it back into my room in the nick of time before I was called to come out!

I remember with great fondness that one of our favorite activities in England was to build a big bonfire once a year, in preparation for Bonfire Night. This is celebrated in England on November 5th and it is a popular night of tradition in England. Many bonfires are built and a Guy Fawkes dummy is placed on the top of each bonfire which is set on fire on November 5th. To make our Guy Fawkes dummy we would stuff old pants and a shirt filled with other old clothing and then we would attach the stuffed shirt and pants together. Lastly, we would sew a fake head to the top of our Guy Fawkes dummy. This was a night of great excitement for all youngsters and we would compete against other neighborhood kids to try to build the biggest and most impressive bonfire in the region. On this night of great fun, the adults made treacle toffee and baked potatoes wrapped in aluminum foil for everybody.

In the weeks prior to Bonfire Night we would build a secret camp inside our bonfire after it was built. This was our tradition, year after year. We would have a secret entrance camouflaged on the bonfire and an elaborate hollow space inside the bonfire, complete with carpet, couch and comfortable chairs which we had collected from the refuse piles of various households. We had such a reputation for collecting these items that many kind neighbors would save furniture for us that they planned to discard, as Bonfire Night approached. We would all meet secretly inside our camouflaged camp and we would hang out there and hold our 'administrative' meetings.
One day, when we were inside our bonfire, a vagrant actually urinated on our bonfire while we were inside it! He obviously did not realize we were inside the bonfire because we had made sure our presence was well concealed!
Sadly, our annual tradition of housing our camp inside our bonfire came to an abrupt halt once we realized some rival neighborhood kids in the area were setting fire to bonfires before November 5th.
We were aware we could be burned alive if our bonfire was set ablaze by some kids who did not realize we were actually inside the pile of wood! Bonfire Night wasn't as much fun after this, but we

had all agreed we couldn't continue to have a secret house inside our bonfire because it was too dangerous.

Chapter 3 – A Terrifying Climb

As I entered my teen years, I began to separate from Mouse and his friends and I instead began to socialize more with Angela, a friend who was both a classmate and a local neighborhood friend. My last hurrah with Mouse and his friends was very exciting. I took a little boy I was babysitting to the park. I saw Mouse and the others while I was there. They seemed pretty disgruntled that they had not seen much of me lately and this was because I had been with Angela more often. They told me they were going to climb Saint Elphin's church and they bet me I would be too scared to go with them. It was true that I was not anxious to partake in this particular activity and so I decided to call their bluff and tell them I would gladly go with them but they would have to wait for me while I took the little boy home. I was confident that they would not want to wait for me, but unfortunately, I was wrong. They told me they would wait until I returned so we could all climb the church together! I was not one to want to give the appearance that I was chicken and so I went home to change into jeans after I had taken the little boy home. I returned to the park, ever so hopeful that they would have left without me, but I had no such luck. They were all waiting and we made our way over to the church. We had been told previously that this church has the third highest steeple in England. I looked up at the church and saw it was surrounded by scaffolding because it was being sand-blasted. We began to climb. Because of my short stature, I could only just reach from one bar of the scaffolding to the next. This was no easy task for me and my hands were moist with sweat because I was nervous. As we neared the steeple, I glanced down and I saw a man walking with his dog on the church grounds. The man appeared to be the size of a pinhead! I was thankful the man did not look up and see us on the scaffolding because I know he would have called the police and we would have been in serious trouble! I was relieved when we reached the steeple and we climbed in through a dusty old window. The place looked eerie, and there were many pigeon carcasses scattered around on the dusty, unkempt floor. We knew we could take the staircase to get down but we were concerned that we could get caught if we went down this way. We decided, instead, to climb back out through the window and then down again, along the scaffolding bars. Again, I could only just reach from bar to bar due to my small frame. My hands were once again moist with sweat because I was gripping as tightly as I could onto the metal scaffolding bars. I was all too aware that with one slip, I could fall to my death. I breathed an enormous sigh of relief when I finally stepped down off the scaffolding onto the soft green grass of the church grounds. Thankfully, I was still in one piece, and so was everybody else.

Meanwhile, at school, Angela and I were friends with classmates, Jane and Diane. Jane was tall and slender while Diane was short and petite. Angela had a heavier build and I was short with curves. We were all in the bright student 'A' stream classes but we weren't studious, serious types. One day, we decided to skip class and play a game we made up and called "Miss World" in an empty classroom. Each of us strutted across the classroom pretending to be gorgeous and we each hoped to be picked to be Miss World by the three judges, who were, of course, ourselves. Well, it was great fun. That is, until we tried to leave the classroom to attend the next lesson. This next lesson was being taught by our home room teacher and she had marked us present earlier that morning and therefore she would be expecting us to show up for her class. This meant, of course, it was imperative that we get to our next class without delay or otherwise be busted. We tried to leave the empty classroom but realized we could not leave without being seen by Miss Newby, the music teacher, as she played thunderously on her piano with gusto. Her classroom door was wide open and it adjoined our empty classroom! It was impossible for us to leave the building through the doorway without Miss Newby seeing us and if we did try to leave she would immediately know we had been up to no good because the classroom should have been empty. We had no choice but to concoct plan B. We decided we had to climb out through one of the very small windows in the classroom. Diane went first because she was the smallest. Then I squeezed out through the window with a little difficulty. Jane went after me and she had to go through a few twists and turns in the window to get through it successfully. Angela went last and we were concerned, with good reason, that she would get stuck in the window. She was certainly a tight fit in the window and the expression 'lemon squeeze' comes to my mind. We all helped her squeeze through the small window by giving her an extra push and she plopped onto the ground then quickly stood up and dusted herself off. We rushed to class and arrived with precious seconds to spare. We entered the classroom and sat quietly at our desks, trying our best to appear as inconspicuous and innocent as possible.

One evening after school, Angela and I were at my house. We were bored and we wanted something interesting to do. After all, we never did our homework and so we had a lot of free time to ourselves to do nothing. I began to write comical limericks that included amusing details about each of our teachers, such as 'Miss Stone' and 'thin as a bone' for example. Angela and I were literally rolling over on the floor and our stomachs ached because we laughed so much. The limericks were hilarious because they described many of our teachers in a less than complimentary manner. We concocted an exciting idea; we decided to use these limericks to create a show to raise money for our school. We met with our headmistress to seek approval for the idea. We were disappointed because she seemed most unimpressed with our paperwork which detailed ideas for the show. I am sure this is because Angela and I were considered capable students that put forth no academic effort, so why should the headmistress go out of her way at this time to encourage us? She did, however, give us permission to press on with the idea for the show, since it was a benefit to raise money for the school which, she told us, was an honorable idea. We scheduled a date for the show and we designed signs and posted them around the school to advertise the event, which we named 'The Big Time Comedy Show'. Angela and I received a lot of interest from fellow students who were excited and wanted to audition to perform in the show.

Our school was partitioned equally to separate the girls and boys however the assembly hall was shared by both genders but at different times of the day. The windows of the assembly hall were covered with brown paper so that the boys could not become distracted and see over into the girls' side of the school. The 'Big Time Comedy Show' was to be held in the assembly hall of the school. We had an admission fee for the show and on show day it was exciting because we had an excellent attendance of female students and school staff-members. We reserved the front row for the headmistress and teachers. The teachers fortunately saw the humor in the lighthearted and yet discourteous limericks about themselves. My mongrel dog had ginger-colored fur with a white stripe down to her pink nose, hence her name, Chalkey. She was decked out with a pink ribbon around her neck. She was the star of the show because she performed tricks for treats, such as 'roll over' and 'jump over the stick'. Lorraine McGlinchey knelt beside a chair on which Chalkey was seated, and she sang sweetly into Chalkey's ear, "Oh It's Fun Being A girl". The audience loved it and they became very excited when I threw candy out into the crowd.

All was going well, that is, up until the 'pretend' striptease act. We were not able to locate appropriate striptease music, and so a group of us improvised and stood behind the open stage curtain to sing the tune to striptease music loudly as Lorie Stiles began to take off her clothes on stage. I could see boys peering at the stage through the edges of the windows which were not completely covered with the brown paper. The headmistress and the teachers stood up and left the assembly hall in disgust, appearing alarmed at what they had been witnessing. The zipper on Lorie's dress became stuck and several of us ran out on stage to assist her. Lorie was able to continue her striptease act as planned, down to her bikini, at which point she stopped and threw more candy out to the audience before taking a bow.

By the end of the show I was satisfied because I felt we'd had a successful show, despite the teacher walkout, and we had raised money for the school. The students had all enjoyed the show, even the boys who had eagerly peered in through the precious tiny portions of uncovered windows!

After the show, Angela and I placed the money we had raised into a decorated cardboard box and we tied it around Chalkey's neck. We proceeded to the office of our headmistress and we humbly presented the box to her. She looked at us disapprovingly but then she graciously accepted the money. Surprisingly, we received no reprimand from her. I think she considered that our intentions were good despite our apparent deficiency in good judgment due to lack of chronological maturity. She asked that in future we warn her ahead of time of 'inappropriate' show content. I explained that the content of the show was listed in the written materials which we had provided to her when we first sought permission to have the show. At this, I thought it best that we leave her office promptly since I recognized the disapproving look in her eye!

Chapter 4 – Gender Rebellion

Meanwhile, at school I became dissatisfied with regard to my choice of classes. For example, I wanted to take a class in woodwork because I thought it would be useful to me and also enjoyable. I was disappointed to be informed that the woodwork class can only be taken by boys. Girls, on the other hand, had to choose either needlepoint or domestic science. I initially chose to take needlepoint but then I changed my mind and so I begged Mrs. Hossop, the domestic science instructor, to allow me to take her class instead. She was flattered by my interest in her class and so she made special arrangements to allow me to transfer from needlepoint into her class. Unfortunately, once I was in her class I rebelled. This is because I was becoming increasingly disturbed at the emphasis to direct domestic work to females, both at home and at school. I came to the conclusion that boys were treated much more fairly than girls and I began to express my dissatisfaction with this fact. I did not realize at the time that there were many other individuals in the world, mostly women, who also considered this emphasis on traditional roles to be grossly unfair to females. I went on in Mrs. Hossop's class to earn a pathetic 30% grade for my domestic science project. This project had been graded by instructors that were independent from our school. I think Mrs. Hossop was so appalled at my effort to under achieve in her class that she crossed out the three points out of ten possible points awarded to me by the instructors who were independent of our school, and she awarded me a generous two and one half points out of ten instead! I was thrilled with this low grade at the time because I considered it symbolic of my dissatisfaction with the school's traditional academic program. My poor grade was a badge of honor and I was proud of it! Earlier in the year, when Mrs. Hossop still trusted that I was putting forth my best effort, she had assigned me the important task of baking cookies for the annual staff meeting. She was positively livid when I sheepishly informed her, just minutes before the important staff meeting was to begin, that I had burned all of the cookies! She was indignant and she behaved as if she thought I had burned the cookies on purpose! (Contrary to what you might think, this really had not been an intentional act on my part.) By the end of the school year, Mrs. Hossop was very snooty and she refused to look at me or even acknowledge my presence. I think I had become a thorn in her side and she was anxious to have me out of her class. I actually felt guilty and sorry that I had messed her around so much. Of course, Mrs. Hossop did not have a psychology degree and she therefore could never have understood my complex emotions or the underlying reasons for my apparently inconsiderate behavior. She was clueless that I was behaving badly in school, not because I disliked her or her class, but because I was rebelling against being forced to accept a stereotypical female role. This was a role I wanted to shed; much like a snake sheds its skin and replaces it with a new one. However, I wasn't being allowed to shed an old role and replace it with something new. I wanted to learn a new skill in school but the school would not allow this simply because of my gender. I was extremely resentful towards the school at this point. I had more than enough experience cooking and cleaning already because I had to do plenty of this type of work at home. What I really needed was some of those interesting traditional male gender classes, such as metalwork and woodwork. It was sheer stupidity to keep me out of those classes simply because of my gender and I was very unhappy with the specific rules that were keeping me from classes I would actually enjoy.

I never expected to be a good math student, probably because I had always been told that girls are not good at math whereas math always comes naturally to boys. I therefore understood this to be fact. As a result I was intimidated by math and I concluded I could never be good at it. Surprisingly, I did perform well in math initially in secondary school, probably because my friends were fairly serious students, and so I followed suit. The math instructor would assign our class a list of problems to solve and she would complete the problems herself at the same time that the students were completing the problems. My three friends, Jane, Angela, Diane and I decided to compete against the teacher, just for fun, and we would hurry to solve all of the problems before she was able to complete them. We would then race up to her desk, completed problems in hand. She obviously did not appreciate our enthusiasm and she would appear quite flustered that we had completed the problems before she had completed her problems, time after time. To solve her unpleasant dilemma, the math instructor had the four of us transferred into the advanced math class. Unfortunately, the class was already well into trigonometry and Jane and Diane, in particular, had difficulty picking up the math concepts midway and so they were moved back into the regular math class. Angela and I were kept in the advanced math class and I was disappointed because I missed my previous math instructor very much. I didn't at all care for the advanced math instructor. He had a reputation for rubbing his arms up against the female students' breasts as he went around the classroom to check our work. I was always careful to shield my chest from him! I was quite the prankster also. When the teacher turned away from me, I held up a white postcard on which I had written the word, 'WUR' in large letters. As soon as the teacher turned to face me to see what the class was giggling about, I would quickly hide the postcard. The class was curious to know what the definition of the word, 'WUR' was, but I wouldn't give away my secret. The truth was; it was a nonsense word that meant absolutely nothing!

Even though the teacher never caught me holding up the postcard, he probably knew I had something to do with the class giggling. When Angela and I asked him for permission to be absent from his class so we could prepare the school tents for an upcoming school trip, he seemed eager to grant us permission. We assured him that we would complete his class work during our own free time, even though I expect he knew we had no intention of doing this. I am sure the teacher was looking forward to having us out of his classroom so that he could have some peace and quiet back! At the end of the class year he smugly told Angela and I that he doubted we could pass the final examination that was to be graded independently of the school. He did not appear at all pleased when, despite his prediction, both Angela and I passed this exam with a respectable average grade! Not bad for a couple of tent stitchers!

Chapter 5 – Lung Cancer

I was still fifteen years old when I was told my dad had lung cancer. He had developed some chest pain and then he began to cough up blood. He was a two pack a day smoker and he had tried to quit smoking several times. My mother told me that she had quit smoking when I was a toddler in order to save money. When she would warn my dad of the perils of continuing to smoke he would respond by saying, "We all have to die of something." I'm sure that he never thought that his time to die would be when he was just forty six years of age! He had always had such a colorful personality and he was a handsome man. He loved to sing and play our electric organ with our front door wide open for all our neighbors to enjoy. He was passionate about politics and he often made his dissatisfaction with various government policies apparent by writing on large postcards in bold red ink and then mailing the postcards off to Number Ten Downing Street. When I was younger, I worried that policemen would come to our house to handcuff my dad and drag him off to prison to punish him for his bold political opinions. It is frightening to realize that in many oppressed countries this actually does occur.

I was deeply saddened to witness my dad lose his attractive mane of thick, dark hair due to the lung cancer treatment. He isolated himself to his bedroom because he was embarrassed to be seen without his hair. One day, I took some lunch to his room. He told me to sit on a chair next to his bed in his room, because he wanted to speak to me about my boyfriend, Ian. I had met Ian at an evening art school class and he had asked if he could walk me home. We then started to see each other on a fairly regular basis. Ian was a drummer in a heavy-rock band. Dad confided in me that even though he liked Ian, he said he was concerned that Ian was content to be just another 'spoke in a wheel' and that he would never amount to anything special. Dad told me he wants somebody special for me; somebody nice and with ambition to be successful in life. I felt truly honored that my dad considered me to be so special! My dad rarely spoke to me so intimately about my personal life and about my future, and so I considered this conversation to be of special relevance to him and I therefore decided I must consider it carefully. Retrospectively, this discussion became even more significant, as I realized it was actually his dying wish for me. I continued to see Ian, off and on, for a couple of years after my dad's death. Ian and I became soul mates, and I still remember him fondly. He helped me through some difficult times, and I like to think that I also helped Ian through some rough times. For example, I remember a night when Angela and I stopped by at a club intending to surprise Ian and his friend, Keith. Ian came out of the club, walking unsteadily, and he announced with slurred speech, "Hi! I'm high!" I was very upset, because I hate illicit drugs and the mess they make of peoples' lives, and so I immediately told Ian I never wanted to see him again and I left with Angela. We stopped at Angela's house to pack her overnight bag because she was sleeping over at my house as she often did. When we arrived at my house I saw Ian waiting for me. He asked if he could speak to me and I reluctantly let him walk with me along Willis Street, the next street over from my house. He asked me if I would continue to be his girlfriend. I told him if he would cut his hair short and stop taking drugs I would agree to continue our relationship. He had long dark hair down to his shoulders and this suited his image as a drummer in a rock band. I was taken aback that he was agreeable to no more drugs and even a hair cut. My sister is a terrific hair stylist and she volunteered to give Ian a nice hair cut. His new hair style looked great and Ian actually liked it! About a year later, Ian thanked me for rescuing him from the drug environment. Unfortunately, drugs were responsible for the death of one of his closest friends and he was witnessing the downward spiral direction in the lives of many of his close friends. He told me, "It's not fun for them anymore, and it's very depressing to watch. I'm so thankful you got me out when you did." Likewise, I was thankful Ian was willing to change his behavior when I stumbled across him happy and high as a kite that night.

In August 1974 my father died at home of metastatic lung cancer and that Christmas my mother traveled to America for a much needed vacation and to see her sister, Sylvia who lived in Saxonburg, Pa. While in America she was introduced to Joseph Boldy, a hard working farmer who had never married. Toward the end of her visit to America, Joe surprised my mother when he asked her to marry him. Of course my mother told Joe she needed some time to consider his proposal of marriage. After she returned to England, Joe visited my mother because he wanted to meet her family. Joe came to our house and when I was introduced to him he seemed nervous. I immediately liked Joe. It was obvious to me he was a sincere and honest man. I encouraged my mother to accept Joe's marriage proposal. After all, I explained, I was the youngest of her seven children and I would soon be leaving home. After further consideration, my mother accepted Joe's proposal and she moved to America to live with Joe on his farm.

I desperately fought emotional acknowledgement of the dissolution of my family. I had always been an inherently happy person, and I wanted to remain this way. I remained in denial about my father's death as I continued my usual routine and went about my days, trying to behave as though nothing had changed. I had completed my high school education, but before I had left, my school career counselor had made arrangements for me to apply to a cadet nurse program. Her recommendation to me was that I should attend this program at ages sixteen and seventeen, and then at age eighteen, she recommended that I enter into a three year student nurse program to become a Registered Nurse at age 21. I was fortunate to have this career counselor because, quite frankly, at this particular time in my life, I simply had no personal solid plans for my future. I took the entrance exam for the Cadet Nursing Program. During the test, I realized the math was more advanced than any that I had taken. Rather than simply give up, I decided to be creative and conjure up my own solutions to the math problems. I was surprised that I actually finished the test early! I completed the example problems on the front page because I was not allowed to leave the classroom early and I needed something to do. About two weeks later I was called into the matron's office. She smiled warmly and she and two men who appeared very formal dressed in suits shook my hand and congratulated me. I was told that I had passed the test and I was accepted into the program. The two men left the room and the matron then seemed to undergo a sudden unpleasant personality transformation. She frowned and told me she thought I was over-confident because I had completed the example problems on the front page of the test. She warned me not to be smug because the program would be a challenging experience. There were several other people present who then went on to congratulate me. I had not been aware this was a big deal until I was told I was the only student from my school that had passed the test and was accepted into this program. I became uncomfortable when I saw students outside the matron's office who were crying because they had not been accepted into the program. These students had obviously put their hearts and souls into applying to this program, whereas I had simply been guided by my counselor, who told me what to do and when to do it. For the next several years, despite the warning I had received from the matron to lose my 'smugness', I continued to drift, much like when a small tree branch is carried aimlessly atop some rapid river water. It was clear I had yet to find some meaningful purpose for my life.

I moved out from my family's home after my father's death and I moved into a house which belonged to an elderly woman named Mrs. Sherburne. She was an eighty-eight year old widow whose family wanted somebody reliable to stay at the house in case she fell and also to be company for her. By this time, each of my family members had experienced their grieving process and then recovered. It was at this time that I finally acknowledged the major changes which had recently taken place in my life. Specifically, my father was dead, my mother was now living in America, and my family was now dispersed. Only now did I allow myself to experience the inevitable depression which I had been desperately trying to avoid. By this time however, I was alone and there was nobody for me to turn to for the emotional support that I needed. My life was vacant and hollow. I was alone and isolated, but I had never been one to seek out support and help in the past, and I had no intention of seeking out emotional support now. This, for me would be a sign of personal weakness, and I preferred to 'tough it out' and get through it alone without acknowledging my vulnerability to another person. I cried often, wondering where my not so distant, happy and carefree world had disappeared to. I was fortunate in that my first ever experience with depression was short-lived. I was truly grateful for my capacity to reject any desire to prolong self pity and I quickly mustered up the inner strength to bounce back from the depths of depression and reclaim my usual vibrant, happy and worry free life.

Chapter 6 – Cadet Nurse

At age sixteen, I started my training as a cadet nurse. Each morning I would take the bus from Mrs. Sherburne's house to the hospital or to the college. I worked in the hospital two days a week where I ran errands for the various nursing departments to which I was assigned. I wore an 'attractive' salmon-pink colored uniform with flat black shoes and a nurse's cap. As cadet nurses we attended the local community college three days a week to prepare for the nursing school. I earned a decent wage to work as a cadet nurse and my tuition cost for nursing school was the responsibility of the government. This was the norm in England. I resumed my carefree and active social life. I never studied and I did not recognize or appreciate the enormous value of my education because it was handed to me on a silver platter, so to speak, by the government. I was totally unaware of how fortunate I was to be the recipient of my nursing education without incurring any debt. On the other hand, the Vietnamese students in my nursing program were extremely serious about their work. I was curious why they were so strikingly different from most of my English friends in that they were outwardly diligent and conscientious. I was curious at the time why there was this striking difference between the Vietnamese nursing students who were in the country temporarily from their native country and the English students. It wasn't until I moved to America that I came to understand a significant and interesting reason for the behavioral difference between the Vietnamese students and the English students and this is because I personally experienced a significant difference in entitlements between England and America. Specifically, when I attended college in America, the silver platter was gone; in fact, there was not even a paper plate to be found, the entitlements were all gone.

I completed the cadet nursing program after two years and I entered into the three year student nursing program as planned. I was now eligible to enter the nurses' residence since I was eighteen years old. My room in the residence building was small but I proudly decorated it with posters I had obtained from our local cinema which advertised current movies. I rarely saw Angela or Ian anymore and I met new friends in the nursing program. On week nights we would frequent the dance club within the hospital grounds, and we would often hire a bus on weekends to take a group of student nurses to the local dance club in Manchester. I was an avid dancer and it was also terrific exercise. The other nursing students told me that I was known to be a good dancer. I would nurse one glass of lager beer all evening so that it would last. I would stay up on the dance floor and dance until the club closed. Most of my friends preferred to sit and chat amongst themselves at a table. I would become restless if I sat at the table with them even for a short amount of time. The beat of the music would release pleasurable brain endorphins and then behave like a powerful and irresistible magnet to my body, pulling me up from the table and over to the floor to dance.

One evening after a full evening of dancing, I was sitting outside the nurses' residence with my boyfriend in his car. I asked another nurse, as she entered the building, to leave the entrance door ajar for me so I could enter the residence after her. This was a common practice between the nurses, so that we wouldn't have to call the nurse supervisor to unlock the building. However, I did not enter the building at that time because my boyfriend and I decided to drive to the local store to buy a snack. We then returned to the nurses' residence a little later. The door was still ajar and so I entered the building and retired to bed. The next morning I was surprised when I was called into the matron's office. The matron was unpleasant in her demeanor towards me and she accused me of having a boy in the nurses' residence the prior evening. (It was strictly forbidden for nurses to take their boyfriends into the residence.) She told me a boy had been sighted early the following morning by one of the student nurses as she walked to the common bathrooms. The nurse who had left the front door open for me had told the matron of this because she was being questioned for having had the key to the nurses' residence, and so I was being accused of bringing my boyfriend into the residence. I was furious at the incorrect accusation. The matron obviously did not believe my personal claim of innocence because she recommended that I buy a bike. (She advised me I would need a bike for transportation since I would no longer be able to stay in the nurses' residence because I had broken the 'no boys allowed' rule.) I protested profusely at the accusation and I slammed her door shut in anger as I left her office.

My friends in the nursing program were equally upset that I was being unfairly accused by the matron. I was grateful to have this demonstration of support from my fellow students but then I also had a stroke of good fortune. My friend Madeline, one of the student nurses, also worked for the local taxi service. She did a little private-eye work on my behalf on the side and she found out that Sheena Green, another student nurse in my class, was the apparent culprit. Madeline found out that Sheena's boyfriend called for a cab to pick him up from outside the nurses' residence at about five o' clock on the morning in question. It turned out he had left Sheena's room, and it was he who was seen walking down the hallway. The student nurse who spotted him promptly reported his presence to the matron. Sheena never did confess to the matron that it was her boyfriend who was in the building and not mine. I found it disturbing that she would turn the other cheek while I take punishment for her misdemeanor, all the while knowing I had no home to go to if I was expelled from the nurses' residence. We never did report our findings to the matron. The matron must have done her own further investigation separately and she discovered for herself that the true guilty person was Sheena and not me. Shortly thereafter, Sheena announced she had decided to move out from the nurses' residence to move back into her parent's home. We knew the true reason Sheena was leaving the nurses' residence was because the matron had told Sheena it was time for her to buy a bike because I didn't need one after all!

Chapter 7 – Brave Patients

What follows are some of my experiences as a young nursing student in England. Granted, some readers may not appreciate what is written, but this is my autobiography after all, and therefore, my writings are of the meaningful experiences in my life so far. Before one reads further, let me first apologize for some of the gory and depressing details. These impressions have touched me deeply like nothing else I have since experienced and I feel they have molded me into the compassionate and thoughtful doctor that I am today.

One of my saddest and most memorable experiences in nursing school is that of my patient, Rene Brownling. She was a patient on the gynecologic oncology floor and I was responsible to change her dressings daily. She told me that of all the nurses, she preferred that I change her dressings because I was more thorough compared to other nurses who, she complained, worked hurriedly in order to get to the rest of their work. I would take my time caring for Rene. She was about fifty years old and she and her husband owned and operated a bar. She would smoke a cigarette while I changed her dressings and she would talk to me about her various experiences in life. Rene told me that before she had become ill she had developed a small sore on her vulva (female private part) and that she had waited for it to heal. The sore did not heal; instead it became larger, then it ulcerated and began to drain pus. She visited the doctor after several months and a biopsy of the now large ulcer was performed which unfortunately revealed she had advanced cancer of the vulva. Rene was admitted for cancer chemotherapy but her prognosis by this time was dismal. I would remove the old dressings from her abdomen daily. During the dressing changes, Rene's cancerous pelvis would exude a terrible stench which attracted flies into the area. Sometimes, the stench of the cancer was so overwhelming that I would retch as covertly as possible so as not to embarrass Rene. Fortunately, Rene's pain was relieved by medication, and she would be quite sedate as she smoked her cigarette while I changed her dressing. After I removed the old exudative soaked dressing, I cleansed the red meaty flesh of her pelvis which was being slowly gnawed slowly away by the malodorous cancer. Her pulsatile abdominal aorta was clearly visible to me as it lay against her vertebral bodies. I realized it may not be long now before the cancer erodes through Rene's aorta. Perhaps it would be a blessing, I contemplated, if she simply hemorrhages to death, peacefully and without pain, one night while she sleeps. Rene was grateful each day as I packed her increasingly hollow pelvis with clean, fresh wet dressings. It was rewarding and fulfilling work for me to be able to provide some small comfort to the last days of Rene's life, simply, as Rene told me, because I was nice to her. Despite my compassion for Rene, I was spoken to by the head nurse. She ostracized me for spending too much time in Rene's room. I was troubled by this criticism of my work because I knew the time I spent with Rene provided much needed comfort to her and that it was the nurses who hurried through their work who should be criticized and not me. I was not deterred and I continued to provide Rene with the nursing care I knew she appreciated and deserved, even though this would result in a negative review for me by the particular head nurse on this oncology floor for women. I was satisfied I had provided solace to Rene during some of the last days of her life. Unfortunately, shortly thereafter, I was assigned to a different hospital floor. I returned to visit Rene after my work day and I was alarmed to find her room was empty. The head nurse reassured me that Rene had passed away peacefully earlier that day. I was relieved Rene's suffering was finally over. It had been an unusually long and arduous process for Rene and she had passed away peacefully, as I had hoped she would.

It was on another gynecologic oncologic floor that I met Mary J. She was a pretty 30 year old blonde patient with short wavy hair and a vibrant personality. I met her equally nice husband and her twin six year old boys. Mary was admitted to have surgical removal of a cancerous mass from her one of her adrenal glands. After she recovered adequately from her surgery, we helped her out of bed. As we walked Mary down the hallway, supporting her under her arms, she suddenly cried out in excruciating pain in her hip and she collapsed. We frantically held on to Mary and we grabbed a stretcher as quickly as possible to get her back into bed. Unfortunately, x rays of Mary's hip bone showed a cancerous area in the bone. This spread of cancer to the bone had weakened Mary's hip, and this had caused the bone to snap under Mary's weight. Mary was taken back to the operating room to have an orthopedic surgeon apply some nuts and bolts to the main pieces of bone so that she could resume ambulation as soon as possible. A few days after the orthopedic surgery, I was very concerned because Mary described to me, in graphic, tortuous detail, the entire surgical procedure she had undergone, while she was supposed to have been unconscious. I immediately notified the anesthesiologist of Mary's surgical account to me and he came to Mary's bedside to discuss the experience further with her. He explained to Mary that he had not been able to administer the usual amount of general anesthesia for her hip repair because she had received anesthesia just a couple of days earlier for her initial surgery. He explained further that it was potentially dangerous for her body to be given the full amount or anesthesia again due to a cumulative effect of the medication in her tissues. Still, he explained, he thought he had administered enough medication to make her unconscious and unaware of the procedure. Unfortunately, while Mary appeared to be unconscious, she was in fact fully aware of the entire surgical procedure. She described in accurate detail the long skin incision along her thigh, the removal of her flesh from along the bone, the placement of the metal plate against her thigh bone. She detailed the supports which were hammered into her thigh bone through holes in the metal plate. Unfortunately, Mary also heard a discussion among the surgical staff of what a particularly sad and hopeless case this is because there was already spread of the cancer to the bone. The anesthesiologist was visibly distraught over Mary's horrific experience and he apologized to her profusely. I was impressed that Mary remained positive and pleasant despite these unbearable experiences. She did not become introverted or depressed during her recovery period. On the contrary, Mary demonstrated immense courage throughout her hospitalization and she was up and about within a couple of days of her surgery. As soon as she had recovered sufficiently, Mary was allowed to go home to be with her husband and her twin boys. My memory of Mary will forever be an inspiration to me. My witness of her tremendous bravery was undoubtedly just the beginning of more courage she was going to demonstrate in an effort to reduce the grief that her beloved twin boys and her devoted husband would have to endure over the next few months as her body would succumb to the unforgiving cancerous condition she had innocently fell victim to.

Chapter 8 – Munchausen Syndrome

One morning, as I began my work on the gynecologic surgical floor; there was an interesting situation that developed. I had the responsibility to take the temperatures of each of the patients. One patient had been admitted because she had abdominal pain of unknown etiology. She had undergone about four surgeries on prior admissions to the hospital because her pain persisted, but still no cause for her pain had been diagnosed. She appeared well and she was very friendly and pleasant. When I removed the thermometer from her mouth I did a double take as I read that her temperature was 104.6F! I thought to myself, "Something is not right with this particular situation." I noticed she had a cup of hot tea on her bedside table. I became suspicious she had put the thermometer into her tea to increase the reading on the thermometer to give the appearance that she had a fever. I apologized to her and said there must be a problem with the thermometer and that I would need to retake her temperature. I shook the thermometer down to 94.0F and placed it back under her tongue. This time I stayed with her for the three minutes it takes to get a reliable reading. Sure enough, when I removed the thermometer from her mouth it read only 98.0F! I told the patient the temperature reading and I reported this incident to the head nurse on the floor who in turn reported the details to her doctors. This patient underwent no further surgery for her complaints of abdominal pain. She was discharged from the surgical floor and admitted to the psychiatric unit for treatment of her mental illness which is called Munchausen's Syndrome. This is a serious mental illness, also known as hospital addiction syndrome, in which a person knowingly subjects himself or herself to multiple unnecessary surgeries or medical treatments by falsifying symptoms or medical test results in order to gain attention of some kind. The realization that she had dipped her thermometer into her hot tea to make it appear she had a fever was enough to confirm a psychiatric diagnosis and prevent further unnecessary surgeries. Nurses can be an invaluable asset to help in the diagnosis of patients' conditions and this is a case that I personally came across.

Chapter 9 – Shameful Behavior

I had a disturbing experience during my assignment on the area of the hospital which was assigned for private patients. One of the patients was my age and I knew her vaguely from one of the dance clubs we both frequented. I was told by the head nurse that the patient was pregnant (again!) and she was admitted to the hospital to have her pregnancy terminated. It was a highly secretive situation and hospital staff employees were told to be 'closed mouthed' about her admission. She certainly did not behave as if she belonged to a wealthy family, but I concluded her family must be affluent because of the extreme importance placed on keeping her situation confidential. I was assigned to attend the termination of her pregnancy and this was scheduled to take place in her hospital room. I was present with other staff members in the patient's room when the doctor walked in to begin the procedure and he injected the patient intravenously with some medicine. The patient's father seemed gruff and bossy and he paced impatiently around her hospital room. He behaved in an arrogant manner and as if he thought he was more important than any other person that was present. He was assured by the doctor that things would begin to occur soon and, sure enough, it wasn't long before the patient began to writhe in pain and cry out loud due to abdominal pain and this pain continued for several hours. Suddenly, a gush of tissues and bloody fluid appeared on the bed sheets, and I was shocked when a pink, perfectly formed, beautiful baby boy plopped out from the writhing patient's vaginal orifice and landed inside a large, cold, stainless steel bowl. The baby could move, and he was warm with open eyes. He was promptly carried from the room in the large, cold bowl. I was emotionally shaken by this whole experience and I was unprepared for the next incident. There was another gush of bloody tissues from the young patient's body. I was further shaken as she produced yet another beautifully formed, soft and warm, pink baby boy. I was helpless to intervene as the second infant was scooped up and placed into another cold, stainless steel basin. The staff member quickly scurried out of the room, carrying the warm and pink baby boy in the large, cold bowl. The patient expressed relief that her pain had ceased and she was ignorant that she had delivered impeccably formed twin baby boys. She was comforted by a staff member and given a sedative so she could rest since her torturous physical ordeal was now over. I walked to the lab area on the floor and I was distraught because I witnessed the employees of the hospital permit these two beautiful baby boys slowly succumb to death over the next several hours because vital fluid and nutrition which was needed to sustain life was withheld. I was under twenty years of age and I was greatly disturbed by what I had just witnessed. The atmosphere on the hospital floor was tense and the normally playful staff members were visibly stressed over this sobering and upsetting assignment.

It was not even a week later that I saw the patient in a popular local dance club. She made her way over to me and she was smiling. She had an alcoholic beverage in her hand and she whispered into my ear. She requested that I speak nothing of the incident to her boyfriend because he was not aware she had ever been pregnant. I reassured her I would not speak to anyone of her hospitalization because I had a professional responsibility to maintain patient confidentiality. How sad, I thought to myself, this young female was unaware she had produced two perfectly formed, baby boys and they had died because nourishment was withheld. I found it disheartening that childless couples, who desperately want a child, were not given the opportunity to adopt these two beautiful baby boys. For some senseless reason, these two perfectly formed and viable baby boys had not been provided nourishment, and for this senseless reason alone, they each took their last breath.

Chapter 10 – First Visit to America

My mother and I wrote to each other regularly and we arranged that I would visit her in America during my first year of nursing school. My flight to America was uneventful. I arrived at the airport in Pittsburgh and my mother and my stepfather, Joe, both greeted me with hugs before we made our way to Saxonburg. Joe is the proud owner of 200 beautiful acres of farmland and he has added a lake to supply water to the farmland and also for recreational purposes. My mother's sister, Sylvia, lived on property next to Joe's farm. At the time of this first visit to America, Sylvia arranged for Phil Hoffman, the son of a minister at her church, to show me the scenic highlights in Pittsburgh. Phil called to speak to me on the phone and we talked for about an hour. Phil told me later, after he hung up the phone that he told his mother, "I could hardly understand a word she said!"

Later that evening Phil came to the farm to meet me. My mother wanted me to change into, 'some nice clothes' for Phil's visit. It was apparent that my mother was pleased about this meeting and I was reluctant to change, because I had a natural inborn stubborn streak. When Phil arrived at the farm, my initial impression was that he was a handsome, blue eyed and polite blonde young man. I invited him to sit at our kitchen table to talk with me and my stunningly beautiful sister, Jaye. Phil and Jaye talked for most of the evening and Phil told me later that he enjoyed talking with Jaye and he concluded I was very shy because I was quiet.

Before Phil had left that evening, he had arranged to take me out to show me some highlights in downtown Pittsburgh the next day. When he failed to appear for our date the next day I was quite unhappy. However, I smiled and I was relieved when I saw his yellow Hornet driving up to the house, albeit, one hour late. It turned out that Phil and I had got our times confused: I thought he had said he would come by to take me to Pittsburgh one hour earlier then he had apparently said. I laughed as I explained to him that I thought he had stood me up on our first date! Phil took me to Pittsburgh that evening and we rode up Mount Washington on the Duquesne Incline. We ate at a nice restaurant before riding back down on the incline. We had an enjoyable evening together but I actually had to suggest to Phil that he sit closer to me because he was seated on the opposite side from me on the incline! I promised Phil that I would not bite him if he sat on my bench seat and he promptly moved closer to me! As our days together increased in number, Phil became more and more at ease with me. I had been told numerous times that I am very easy to talk to and that I put a person at ease because I have a friendly personality. After several dates, Phil confided in me and said he was more comfortable with me than he had been with any of his past girlfriends. I enjoyed my dates with Phil because I, likewise, found Phil to be friendly and easy to talk to. I especially liked that Phil preferred a natural appearance. I was accustomed to applying cosmetics onto my face in England before daring to be seen in public. Phil told me he actually prefers no make-up! He would request, "Please, don't put that stuff on your face. You have such a nice complexion; it is a shame to cover it up with make-up." Phil also exposed me to many spectacular places as we traveled around, enjoying the scenery. On one of our outings we went spelunking in the Laurel Caverns. We explored the caverns without a tour guide and we were successful in finding our way out of the caverns uninjured! Exploring alone in this fashion without a tour guide is no longer permitted. All too quickly, my three week vacation in America came to a close. Phil drove me to the airport and we promised each other we would keep in touch through the mail regularly after I had returned to England.

Chapter 11 – Marriage Proposal

After I returned to England, the employees at the nurses' residence were very excited because I began receiving mail from my new American boyfriend. Small packages were arriving daily from America and the employees were interested and smiling as I would pick up my package daily after work. It seemed that anyone who knew me was curious regarding any news I would share with them about America and my new boyfriend. I suppose I lived in a small town where interesting news was hard to come by and my situation at this particular time was interesting news! Phil and I grew closer through our correspondence in the mail, and then at Christmastime, I received a surprise in the mail. It was a round trip plane ticket to take me to America! I later found out that Phil had sacrificed his beloved motor cycle so he could see me again!

Christmastime arrived and I flew back to America. Phil greeted me at the airport and we traveled together to the farm. I had made arrangements to remain in America for a couple of weeks. One evening during my visit, Phil and I went to the movies. Before we went to the theater, Phil escorted me into a jewelry store and then he asked me to marry him as we began to look at rings. I was uneasy with this proposal of marriage in a jewelry store because it gave me the impression that Phil thought a diamond ring might play a role to possibly coax me into accepting his marriage proposal. In actuality, nothing could be farther from the truth. Simply put; material possessions are not and never will be as important to me as expressions of love and respect. I therefore said no to Phil's marriage proposal. Phil became very quiet. I was disturbed that I had upset him so much. Therefore, during the movie, 'The Return of the Pink Panther', I turned to Phil and I spoke quietly into his ear, "Yes, I'll marry you." I was relieved because he was no longer despondent and we both enjoyed the movie because the awkward tension between us was no longer present.

Over the next few days, I told Phil repeatedly that I was concerned my decision to get married was wrong. I wanted to feel more positive about my decision. His reply to me was that this is perfectly normal. He told me he expected that I would never be sure about whether or not I should get married. I explained to Phil that my impression of marriage for a female is that she gets married and then she dies! My observations had been that females enjoyed their lives only when they were single. I had reached the conclusion that once a female is married she is abandoned and is left alone at home by her spouse. She is expected to take care of the family and the home while her spouse believes he is entitled to continue to go out and frolic with his friends. This was my impression of expectations in my home town of Warrington, England. I told Phil I had seen this situation play out time and time again. Therefore marriage seemed to be an unfortunate and unfair trap for females. Needless to say, I was very guarded with respect to marriage and my subsequent future. I wanted to maintain my satisfying life and my independence. I appreciated that one wrong decision, such as the decision to get married, could result in a future filled with regret. Phil assured me that things would be different in our case. He told me that marriage can, and should be, the beginning of a wonderful and enjoyable life together. I was skeptical and I was still far from eager to be married. Phil did a lot of arm twisting on multiple occasions as he worked hard to try to convince me we could have an enjoyable future together. I finally agreed to officially accept Phil's proposal of marriage. I was still lukewarm about the idea of marriage because my overriding concern was one of what I stood to lose, over what I stood to gain.

I returned to England with an engagement ring on my finger and my friends were excited about my English-American romance. I too enjoyed the excitement and it was a fact that I actually wanted the course of my life to take some unusual twists and turns. I think the reason for this was because of the small and ordinary little town in which I was raised. In this small town, the ordinary people were content to do the usual 'same old, same old' with their lives. For some reason, however, the thought of following this 'same old, same old' routine with my life disturbed me a great deal. I wanted to do something other than 'ordinary' with my life although I did not know exactly what it was I wanted to do with my future. I knew I did not want to pursue the same old mundane routine that I witnessed the families around me practice. I therefore found the current departure from standard events in my life to be energizing. I found it odd that the majority of the population preferred to fit into the standard and ordinary molds within society. For me on the other hand, and for individuals like me, an unknown and uncertain course during one's lifetime was exhilarating and intriguing. The unknown and uncharted course for a life was a desirable goal for me.

I wasn't at all sure why Phil wanted to marry me. We were vastly different from each other. Academics had never been important to me whereas Phil had straight A's throughout school. I was an avid dancer whereas Phil 'sweated bullets' if he even thought about having to dance! I wondered how our relationship would avoid turmoil. Phil and I were told shortly after we were married that his father had expressed to some that he had misgivings about our marriage. I expect Phil's father was disappointed in Phil's choice of me as his spouse because I was not interested in his preaching. The more his father came to know me the more it was evident that Phil would not be able to put me into my 'rightful place'. This rightful place, as Phil's father would try to convince me, was subservient to the male.

Phil's father and I did not see eye to eye at all! He attended church almost every day of the week. The church he attended was a fundamentalist Baptist church that preached hell, fire and brimstone. He repeated many times over to me, "God rules over Jesus, Jesus rules over man, and man rules over woman." We would have discussions about such 'important' issues at his church as the requirement that the female members of the church wear dresses and not pants. I thought this was a ridiculous requirement and I, of course, expressed my sentiment on this topic to Phil's father. Phil and I told Phil's father that during the time this was written in the Bible, the term 'britches' was used to describe any garment that covers the pelvis and hip area. In other words, we explained to Phil's father that contrary to his belief, the Bible does not insist that men wear pants and women wear dresses. The Bible merely indicates that both men and women should dress respectfully. We expressed to

40

Phil's father that these more specific and seemingly ridiculous rules are created from mans' erroneous misinterpretation of the writings in the Bible. We said further that these rules vary from church to church depending upon each congregation's own interpretation, or more commonly, misinterpretation of the writings in the Bible. We were, quite frankly, fed up of all these different interpretations from church to church. One of Phil's father's favorite quotes when he had no logical rebuttal left to give to us after we had challenged his questionable logic supposedly taken directly from the Bible was, "God says it; I believe it; that settles it!" Then that would be the end of any further discussion on that particular subject for the rest of the day!

It is true that Phil was not at all like his father. Before our marriage, I told Phil of my expectations during our discussions about our future together. I told him not to expect to sit lazily in a reclining chair with his feet up after he arrives home from work while I cook and clean in the kitchen. Likewise, I told Phil I would work very hard to meet him halfway in roles that are traditionally handed to the male. I expressed my disdain for stereotyping of genders. I told Phil I especially do not appreciate the expression, "The man is the head of the household". By the same token, I find the commonly expressed opinion, "She has him wrapped around her little finger," to be equally disrespectful to the spouse. I explained I find this mindset irritating, underhanded and demeaning. I observed that the most successful marriages are the ones that display mutual respect for each other and that recognize two heads are better than one for most decisions within a marriage.

While I was on a roll discussing my philosophy with Phil as it pertains to marriage, I confessed to Phil that I would be perfectly content not to have any children. I was relieved when Phil told me that he too was comfortable with this decision. We also discussed our last names and I was disappointed when Phil told me it was important to him that I take his last name. He told me his parents would be very upset if I did not take his name and he said he did not want to offend his parents. This disturbed me because I wanted to keep my own last name and it seemed unfair that I was expected to give up my name simply because of my gender and so as not to offend his parents! Even though I found it difficult on an emotional level to change my last name, I decided to concede because this was one of the few things that seemed important to Phil, whereas I simply considered the tradition of name changing at the time of marriage to be stupid and unfair. In hindsight, I now realize I should have stood my ground and kept the name given to me at birth. In reality, I suspect it was Phil who would have been upset had I not taken his name and I think Phil's parents would have considered this to be our business and not theirs. If I had kept my own name I am sure Phil may have initially been uncomfortable with my decision but I have no doubt given our more recent conversations on this subject, he would have soon approved wholeheartedly of my decision.

The fact that women traditionally acquire their husband's name after marriage has always seemed irrational to me because it is inconvenient for the female to suddenly change her last name after she is married. If you think about it, after she changes her name she then experiences all kinds of problems. For example, many prior acquaintances can no longer contact her because her name has changed. Additionally, a name change bears significant economic disadvantages for a person. For example, banks will be more interested in relationships with males because their names remain constant. I have given this 'female dilemma' some consideration and I have a suggestion that would be an improvement compared to the current arrangement. In the interest of gender fairness and economic equity there should be no change of name upon marriage for either the male or the female. I suggest that when children are born, baby girls are given the mother's last name and baby boys are given the father's last name. This is a fair arrangement for both genders and the current 'female dilemma' is solved! Some countries already have similar last name arrangements for various reasons. Unfortunately, there are those who will complain this is not satisfactory for various reasons such as, some individuals simply do not like change, or, it is no longer romantic as presented in the romantic novels where, "She becomes Mrs. Jeremy Snodgrass." But there is no doubt that female economics and being practical and fair trumps romanticism. I actually had a heated discussion pertaining to this very subject with a female classmate in my nursing school class in Butler, Pa. I was perplexed and dismayed that this individual did not share my concern about the negative impact the current traditional arrangement places on females and she loudly expressed her desire to maintain the status quo because it is respectful to the male! It is attitudes like this that will keep the current system of inequities in place. I hope at some time in the future my suggestion will become a reality and the social pressure that a female experiences to change her name at the time of her marriage will no longer be present.

After discussing my future plans with Phil, I decided I would leave my nursing program in England before completion and I would move to America. Phil came to visit me in England before I left and we enjoyed a trip to Northern England to see The Lake District and Scotland. Phil seemed so confident about what he wanted; his world never seemed to come anywhere close to my personal world of turmoil and uncertainty. However, for the first time in my young adult life I sensed some stability despite a home in a new country. Phil was encouraging me and providing support along my new life journey. I didn't know it yet but I was about to undergo a significant personality transformation that would surprise my former acquaintances in England.

Chapter 12 – Second Visit to America

Phil and I traveled to the U.S. a day apart because there were no seats remaining on the plane which meant we had to travel separately. I booked a room in the airport hotel because my connecting flight to America was not available until the next day. Phil was concerned I would not wake up in time for the early morning connecting flight. I told him not to worry because I would call the front desk and ask the airport employee to 'Knock me up' in the morning. Phil was alarmed and he explained I would not want to request this of the airport employee! Of course this expression means something entirely different in England than it does in America. At home in England I was accustomed to leaving a note on the door of my room in the nurses' residence with instructions for the employees to wake me up at a certain time each day. Specifically, the note would read "Please knock me up at ... o' clock". When Phil explained the usual meaning of this phrase in America we both agreed this would not be an appropriate request to ask of the airport employee!

I completely shocked my Mother when I arrived the second time to America because I had wanted to surprise her that Phil and I were planning a wedding in the very near future. She was very happy to see me standing on her doorstep with my suitcases. She gave me a big hug and said she wanted to do something special for me. She offered to take me out to shop for my wedding dress; what could be nicer than this? We had a very nice day shortly thereafter and I found a beautiful wedding dress that was on sale for $100 and it fit perfectly!

We were married just six weeks after my arrival to America! Phil's father married us and his mother played the organ in the church. We had two wedding receptions: One was held in the church in the afternoon and no alcohol was present. This was for Phil's side of the family and for the members of the Baptist church because they would have been offended if alcohol was served. The second reception was held in the evening on the farm by the lake. This was for my side of the family because my side of the family would have been offended if alcohol was not served! It was a beautiful warm summer evening and a full moon shone down on the wooden dance floor which was encased by hay bails. Phil and I left our wedding reception before midnight to travel toward Niagara Falls, our honeymoon destination.

After our honeymoon, Phil and I found a place to rent on the second floor of a house in Butler, Pa. The lady who owned the house, Mrs. Adams, lived downstairs. We felt sorry for her because she had no transportation to get to church. She would worship the handsome white suit-clad men as they preached their sermons on television while they collected money from their poverty stricken adoring viewers. After the Sunday services it was reported that the preachers would drive directly to the banks in their fancy limousines to deposit their donations. One Sunday, Phil and I offered to take Mrs. Adams to her church. It was an innocent gesture based solely on our good will, but we had no idea what we were getting ourselves into. The church Mrs. Adams belonged to was a Pentecostal church and we were not familiar with this particular type of church but we expected to experience a normal church service.

When we arrived at the church, Phil, Mrs. Adams and I were escorted into the church and seated. Phil and I were shocked when the entire congregation began to cry and shout out uncontrollably before the service had even begun! We were unnerved when two elderly, heavily made up women seated behind us began to speak 'in tongues'. Phil and I knew the bizarre behavior enveloping us could quickly get out of control but we were unable to escape from the mayhem because we were trapped in the center of the pew. To make matters even worse, our sweet landlady had taken the liberty to whisper into the preacher's ear on our behalf, prior to his sermon, to explain that we are not of any religious persuasion. The preacher must have concluded it was his duty to act on this knowledge. "There are two amongst us who are not saved!" He announced loudly. "Step up here and wash away your sins to be born again!" I was aghast when the entire congregation turned and stared at me and Phil. They were chanting monotonously. Phil and I slid quietly down on the church bench as we tried to hide. As soon as the service was over we bolted from the church and waited for our landlady outside the church in our car. We had not realized our landlady would try to impose her religion on us in such a manner and we moved to a different apartment as soon as we could find an alternative residence after this incident.

It was around this time that I had to apply for permanent resident status in the U.S. The immigration procedure was an unpleasant experience. The immigration officials asked Phil and me for personal details about our relationship, such as, where did we go on our first date and they requested details of our first gifts to each other. I knew all of this was pointless. The immigration officials were following blind standard procedure to ensure that I was not a foreign female merely looking to marry an American male simply to gain entrance into America. In my particular case, my mother could have petitioned to bring me in to this country because I was not married when I arrived here. In other words, the immigration officials could have saved some precious time and energy in my particular case because the standard interrogation procedure was unnecessary.

After the immigration procedure I was granted a permanent visa which meant I could now live in the U.S. as a legal resident. My next task was to learn to drive. It had not been necessary for me to drive in England because the public transportation system is excellent. However, I knew it would be necessary for me to drive in America because this country is huge compared to England. Phil volunteered to teach me to drive and he suggested I learn to drive on a manual stick shift. He told me if I can drive a stick shift I can drive anything. On the day of my driving test I was disappointed because my driving test instructor did not crack a smile on his face. I remember at one point when I stopped appropriately at a stop sign, my knee began to quiver uncontrollably as it rested on the brake peddle. I nervously pressed my two hands down on my knee to attempt to control the tremor of my knee. I looked over at the driving instructor and I smiled and told him I must be very nervous. He did not smile. I think if he had smiled his face would have cracked into thousands of tiny pieces which would have fallen down onto his car seat. His demeanor seemed such that he couldn't care less whether I pass or fail, he was simply there to put in his eight hours of work. I was both relieved and surprised when I was told by my grouchy instructor that I had passed my test. I had managed to get through the test without making a mistake and therefore I did not have to return to repeat the test with this grumpy man. I was very happy!

Chapter 13 – Back to Nursing School

After we moved out from the second floor in our crazy landlady's home, we found an apartment to rent which was located in a small town called Connoquenessing, situated outside of Butler, Pa. Shortly after we moved there, Phil told me he was concerned that I had not completed my nurse training because I came to America to marry him. He said my mother might always blame him if I did not complete my nurse training. I considered what he told me and I decided to apply to nursing school at Butler County Community College (BC3). I was surprised to learn that I would not be given a wage while I attended nursing school. I was even more surprised to learn I would actually have to pay to go to nursing school in this country! I had earned a decent wage while attending nursing school in England. I expressed to Phil my expectation that the nursing school education would be very easy since I will have to pay for the education. I would soon find out that it was quite the opposite!

Judy Schilling was the director of the nursing program. Phil's mother went to the college with me to meet with Judy Schilling to discuss my application to the college. I was very forthright and honest as I told Judy I had never applied myself to do well in school, both in my younger school years and later, in nursing school in England. I told Judy that since I was now married to an Einstein-like genius, I felt it was important that I do well academically, and for the first time in my life I intended to be a conscientious student. I asked that she accept me into the nursing school class even though it was already in session because I was anxious to get started. I did not want to have to wait until the following year to begin nursing school. Judy was extremely accommodating. She must have been impressed by my honesty and she agreed to let me join the nursing school in the second semester because of my two years of experience in nursing school in England. Prior to entry, I was told I had to take a math placement test. I knew this would hold me back because of my limited math background. Judy was kind and arranged a meeting for me with Donald Loomis, an academic director at the college. He too was surprisingly accommodating and told me, "You are going to be a nurse, not a mathematician." He kindly waived the math placement test and allowed me to enter the nursing program without taking it! Judy required that I take a General Psychology course as a prerequisite to enter into the nursing program. Judy arranged that the grade I achieved in the psychology course would be the grade I would be credited with for the entire first semester of the nursing program. It was apparent to me and my family that Judy was giving me a wonderful opportunity to perform well in college. I was grateful to her for her kindness and I intended to keep my promise to her that I would be a diligent student for the first time in my life!

I was very excited to join the general psychology class. However, I was intimidated by a friendly but large student named Gerald. He had a reddish colored beard and he was over six feet tall, which is very tall by English standards. He told me this was his third time taking the psychology class and that this time he intended to pass the course. I somehow concluded from his conversation with me that Gerald must be very knowledgeable in psychology. When I told Phil about Gerald and his expertise in psychology, he burst out laughing. I smiled and gradually 'caught on' to my own intimidation and lack of self-esteem when Phil explained to me what he found so amusing. When I completed the psychology course I was thrilled because I had earned an 'A' in the course and this would translate into an 'A' for the first semester of the nursing program, as promised to me by Judy Schilling. The third time was a charm for Gerald, and he was happy because he did pass the course this time.

Chapter 14 – Political Leanings Discovered

It was around this time that I developed some political interest and I discovered that I had leanings to the right of center. I developed an appreciation for the importance of being a self-made man, or, in my case, a self-made woman. I began to groom a strong work ethic for myself. I came to realize I had never appreciated that I was given a wage by the government while I attended nursing school in England. The nursing education in England never cost me a cent. It was all handed to me on a silver platter and I in turn believed I was entitled to the wage I was given. I was given my income first as a cadet nurse at age sixteen and then as a student nurse when I turned eighteen. At the same time, I put forth minimal effort while I was in the English nursing school. This is because I was paid to obtain my nursing education and I never had to contribute any effort in order to receive it. In turn, my nursing education in England was not meaningful to me. I was not motivated with inner drive to do my best while in nursing school in England and my achievements were therefore mediocre.

When I came to this country and I was not happy to learn I had to actually pay for my education. This was a shock to me! I actually had to pay for my education. Worse yet, I would not receive a wage while I attended the school! This was all very strange to me and I did not know what to make of it all. Still, I needed to complete my nursing education and so I had no choice but to proceed into the new system. I told Phil I expected school to be really easy since I had to pay to go to school. I also found it odd that I was perceived as being fortunate that I was accepted into school in the first place. I became aware of many individuals who were not accepted into nursing school. This surprised me since all applicants were willing to pay for their education but they were having difficulty getting accepted into the program in the first place. I had been accepted into school without any difficulty. It didn't occur to me that I might be bright. Gradually in this new education system in America I began to transform. I found I was now eager and willing to roll up my sleeves and apply lots of elbow grease. After all, I now had to use my own, hard earned cash to pay for my education! It slowly became apparent to me that my education has great value. This is because the financing of my education now came directly from my own pocket and not from the government's pocket! In addition, because I was now aware of the high cost of my education, I worked very hard in school for the first time in my life and I subsequently found I derived immense satisfaction from the fruits of my labor. This was a remarkable difference in my attitude compared to my attitude when I had attended school in England.

I thought back to an earlier time in England and I compared it to my current life in America. I was able to identify a key and significant difference between England and America. I think one can generally agree that in 1975, England was a more socialized country than America. One might erroneously conclude from this that England was more successful at enabling its poverty stricken citizens to use its government welfare system to become independent and successful compared to America. However, my observations as a citizen of England were quite to the contrary. I witnessed poor people on the dole, staying on the dole, and having no incentive to get off the dole. I know this because I personally had able-bodied family members who considered themselves entitled to routinely collect their weekly dole money from the government, year after year after year. Keep in mind, in order to provide for this dole money, the government had to take from the middle income tax-payers. I went on to conclude through my personal comparative experience, first in England, and then in America where far fewer social programs existed, that the existence of these government social programs actually cause the diminution of the inner motivation and initiative of the recipient. Even though the intent of social programs is to help recipients, an excess of generosity to individuals from the government can denude an individual's spirit, inner drive and work ethic because it creates an expectation of government hand-outs. The unfortunate result can be an attitude that begs the question, why should I work when I will be given?

Unbeknownst to me at the time, even I was a victim of exactly this scenario for a short time as I attended nursing school in England. In my case, I was fortunate to be freed from this undesirable entrapment. I was able to escape from the socialized system that promotes mediocrity through entitlements and I came to live in America where I applied so much elbow grease that, I am happy to say, the word mediocrity no longer applies to my life! Unfortunately, two of my brothers in England became entwined in this imprisonment of entitlements. I am sad to have witnessed their unwitting satisfaction with this system of free government financial support because it doused water on the fire inside their bellies to become independent, successful entrepreneurs.

I identify with any political group that encourages an individual to pull him or herself up by the bootstraps, and not wait for money for nothing from the government. I had learned through my own experience that an excess of government generosity and social programs often destroys an individual's initiative to achieve personal accomplishment and achievement. It was now apparent to me that this personal pride may develop only after some financial sacrifice has been experienced in order to first strive for, and then accomplish, one's dreams and aspirations. This is a concept which I find difficult to convey to some types of individuals, such as those that are 'do-gooders'. I am usually unable to convince a do-gooder that taxes should be kept down because social programs can do more harm than good. This is because the do-gooder is usually skeptical of my motivation in stating this fact. For example, the do-gooder usually concludes that I am inherently selfish in my true desire to keep taxes low, and a do-gooder believes such individuals as me simply do not want to help poor people in any way, shape or form. I truly believe do-gooders are genuine but naïve in their quest to help the less fortunate people than themselves.

Sadly, I do believe many politicians are selfishly looking out for number one (themselves). There are many hypocritical comments and broken promises made by the politicians on both sides of the aisle. Also, there are many individuals who vote for selfish reasons because they themselves feed from the public trough of entitlements, and so naturally they want to maintain their government sourced sugar daddy. These voters are not going to sever the umbilical cord that promises them lucrative benefits and pensions even if it is responsible for the demise of their city or state, as we have unfortunately already witnessed in many instances. Personally, I am far from completely aligned with any one party and this is why I consider myself to be positioned to the right of center. I do disregard some of my own personal issues because I believe it is of utmost importance to look out for the preservation of future generations by voting first and foremost to secure the future of this country. I detest war, but I recognize that if attacked we should respond aggressively. If we respond in a spineless manner it signals to enemies that we are weak and vulnerable. We must be strong and mighty in order to thwart as many future terrorist attacks as possible to protect our precious young and our homeland. The naïve prefer to bury their heads in the sand and pretend that evil can be eliminated from the face of the earth; they believe we must simply put forth an effort to understand those that hate us solely because we are not them. I find it disturbing and I fail to understand why the dangers posed by terrorists, whose solitary mission is to destroy us, are not crystal clear to all.

Chapter 15 – I Graduated!

I was very happy to be in college. I had earned an 'A' in my first class in America! I had been accepted into nursing school with advanced placement because I was given six months credit for my nursing experience in England. This meant I could enter the nursing school as I had planned, in January. I was ecstatic! It was apparent that the administrative staff recognized my eagerness to get started. I was very grateful for their kindness and for their willingness to adjust and individualize their usual requirements to meet my needs. I went on to complete my nursing education at the college with an impressive 4.0 G.P.A. I was thrilled that I had succeeded in my quest to perform well at the college. It had been important to me to do well for another reason. I personally felt indebted to both Judy Schilling and to Donald Loomis, because they had placed their trust in my words when I had first applied to their college in the very beginning. I wanted to make good on my words to them that I had a sincere desire to change and to do well in college. Judy Schilling and Donald Loomis had given me the initial support that I needed to undergo my academic transformation; just as Kate Bush writes in her song and then she performs so beautifully, 'Rolling The Ball'. Wonderful teachers like this are responsible for touching the lives of many students in countless positive ways, and I am sure I am just one example of many eternally grateful students. I present myself as one small example in a unique position that was given a leg up in the very beginning, when the help was first needed. Now likewise, we should help those who find themselves in positions that need a helping hand of assistance along with a vote of confidence to help boost their self esteem when it is initially needed.

I was feeling fulfilled when I graduated from nursing school with my Associate Degree in Nursing. I initially joined Phil in the family machine shop because Phil was overwhelmed with an excessive amount of work. I drilled holes into the heads of bolts so that these bolts could be wired down and used in large machines such as aircrafts to keep them from becoming loose during operation. I found this to be, excuse the pun, very boring. Once Phil was caught up with his heavy onslaught of work, we both agreed I should begin my profession as a nurse. I applied to North Hills Passavant Hospital and I began my profession as a nurse on a medical-surgical floor.

I initially worked on the general floor of the hospital for about six months and then I applied to work in the emergency department. My application was accepted even though I lacked the experience usually required of successful applicants to be accepted to the emergency department. It turns out I had a stroke of good fortune because the Medical Director of the emergency department had received a complimentary letter written about me from one of his patients that I had cared for while she was hospitalized. This letter had impressed the medical director so much that he accepted my application to work in the emergency department.

I enjoyed the excitement of the emergency department. However, there were poignant times too. One of the saddest experiences that I recall was a twenty one year old male who had fallen asleep in a drunken stupor sprawled across railroad lines. A speeding train had run over him and severed his leg and he was rushed to our emergency department by ambulance. He was awake and alert as we hurried to run intravenous fluids into his veins as fast as possible to try to keep him alive. He was very brave and pleasant and he even told us a few jokes as we frantically worked to compete against his extensive blood loss. But our efforts were futile. We simply could not keep up with his massive blood loss and we were all distraught and saddened as it became clear we were powerless to save him. The young man died on that day despite our most desperate efforts to keep him alive.

On the flip side, one of my favorite regular patients was the crazy lady who would carry a plastic airway under her watchstrap. She would place the airway into her throat herself whenever she would 'supposedly' start to have a seizure, and then she would pretend to be unconscious. We knew her well and we knew from experience that the seizure was not a genuine one. We had a new nurse join our department and she was an excellent nurse but she was not yet familiar with the antics of our seizure lady. On one occasion, the inevitable occurred. The new nurse saw the seizure lady appearing to have a seizure before her very eyes. The seizure lady gasped for air and stuck the airway down her own throat. She promptly apparently became unconscious on the stretcher moments after what had appeared to the nurse to be a genuine seizure. Naturally, the nurse was alarmed and she apparently could not palpate the patient's carotid pulse. She immediately delivered a powerful precordial thump to the seizure lady's chest, fearing her heart had stopped beating. The patient immediately jumped up and angrily yelled, "Jesus Christ! What the hell are you doing?" The nurse appeared stunned and confused at the time. Once we realized what had just taken place, we took the new nurse off to the side and explained the patient's usual theatrics to her. She immediately understood the patient's unexpected reaction to her precordial thump and found the whole incident amusing. Unfortunately, it wasn't long after this that we received some somber news. Our seizure lady had been instantly killed when she ran in front of a bus during a bout of some erratic behavior.

Another memorable emergency department experience for me was one evening when I was working as a triage nurse. I was sitting at my triage desk when a middle aged man entered our emergency department. He told me he was sent on a mission from God to provide a cure for gonorrhea (a sexually transmitted disease). He went on to say that God had placed a droplet of a chemical on his forehead as he was walking along the street, and he had been instructed by God to come to the hospital to have the droplet analyzed, because it contains the cure for gonorrhea. I decided my best course of action would be to advise the emergency department doctor of the situation. I did not want to vex this patient who, I suspected, suffered from schizophrenia. I knew that when patients with this condition do not take their antipsychotic medication they often lose contact with reality and they may become delusional. The doctor took the man into a patient room and he swabbed the man's forehead to obtain a culture. The man was therefore satisfied he had fulfilled his mission from God. Our emergency department doctor also encouraged the man to schedule an appointment with his Psychiatrist as soon as possible because he had run out of his regular medications.

Chapter 16 – Back to School

One leisurely weekend evening when we were not scheduled to work, Phil and I went out to eat at Perkin's Pancakes family restaurant. I was satisfied because I had finally been able to convince Phil to return to college. Initially, Phil had refused to consider going back to college because he expected that after college he would simply return to his family's machine shop to work, even though he had earned a bachelor's degree. I told Phil that at least he would then have a choice, whereas his only choice at the present time was to work in the machine shop. I wanted Phil to return to college because I knew he possessed a brilliant brain, and I had also been concerned that the family machine shop was not good for his health. I knew it was not a healthy environment because I had also spent a considerable amount of time working in the machine shop until I began to work as a nurse. It was hot and humid in the summer with no air conditioning. In the winter, it was freezing by about 2pm, after the day's allotment of wood had been burned for heat. On one particular day, I remember I was alarmed because Phil was chilled through to his bones when he arrived home from work. It took him over one hour to warm up in bed under heavy blankets. On countless occasions, Phil's father had promised him he would build a new machine shop. When Phil presented suitable areas of land to his father, on which to build a new family machine shop, his father was clearly not interested. Phil became frustrated that his efforts to find suitable land were not taken seriously. Finally, Phil told me he was agreeable to return to college. I was thrilled at his change of attitude because I knew incredible opportunities would be available for his remarkable intellectual capability.

As we discussed Phil's future in college over coffee and pancakes, Phil unexpectedly turned the table on me. We both knew I had done remarkably well in nursing school and I told Phil that I should further my education and become a nurse practitioner after he had completed his college education. Phil took me by surprise when he announced that he thought I should become a doctor. He told me he thought I would be happier if I was able to make my own independent medical decisions rather than having to rely on a supervising physician to approve my decisions. Becoming a doctor had never occurred to me, and yet my husband had complete confidence in my ability to become one. What a turn of events! Phil insisted we could both work and attend college at the same time and he suggested we try doing this for a semester to see how things go. We had already completed payments on a new mobile home we had purchased and so we had no mortgage or rent to pay, and therefore we were only responsible to pay a small monthly amount for the plot of land we had our mobile home on. We concluded by the end of the evening that we could both continue to work and actually return to school concurrently.

I distinctly remember the day Phil went to meet his new college advisor at Slippery Rock State College. When he returned home from the meeting he was no longer reluctant to return to school. In fact, he was now very excited about returning to college because he had learned of a new area of education he could concentrate on that he found particularly interesting. It was called computer science. Phil had decided against his original major in math and physics. As fate would have it, about eighteen months earlier I had bought Phil a new and strange gadget for his Christmas present. It was called a computer. This was available at Radio Shack and my step-father kindly co-signed for the loan so that I could make monthly payments on the very expensive $600 computer. Because of my student status and also due to my lack of credit history, the computer was too expensive for the store to allow me to purchase it alone using credit. When I gave Phil his birthday present, it was a complete surprise to him and I could see that he loved his present. Little did I realize at the time how essential it was that Phil had a computer and that he would go on to enjoy a personally satisfying and highly successful career change!

Meanwhile, Phil asked Ruth, a girlfriend from his past who was now a medical student at the University of Pittsburgh, to arrange a meeting for me with the director of admissions at the medical school. I attended the meeting and I asked the medical director if I would be considered for admission to a medical school if I earned 120 college credits from Slippery Rock State College without a bachelor's degree. I explained to the medical director that once I had completed 120 college credits, a requirement of a bachelor's degree would delay my application to medical school by an additional year. I went on to explain that I had earned 60 credits in nursing school and the basic pre-med requirements would add another 60 credits and this would total 120 credits altogether. The minimum requirement for entrance into most medical schools was 120 college credits, 60 of which had to be from a pre-med curriculum. The medical director was very helpful to me because she confirmed that I would be considered for admission without a bachelor's degree if I had completed the 120 college credits. She then reached under her desk and brought out a small book. She began to flip through the pages, "Hmm, Slippery Rock State College. Now let me see… Yes, here it is! Hmm, this book says Slippery Rock State College is less competitive. If you are serious about getting into medical school then I suggest you go to a more prestigious pre-med college such as this one. I strongly suggest that you come here to the University of Pittsburgh instead of attending Slippery Rock State College." I thanked the medical director for her time and also for her advice and I told her I would take everything she had recommended to me into serious consideration.

Phil and I discussed my options. We decided it would be better if I take classes at Slippery Rock State College and not at the University of Pittsburgh. One of my personal reasons for wanting to take classes at the 'less competitive' Slippery Rock State College was because I did not really expect my desire to become a doctor to materialize. I was well aware that the likelihood of my success was slim to none. I considered I was seriously disadvantaged when compared to other pre-med students because of my weak academic background. I knew that the typical pre-med student was very serious about their future from a young age, and that they had typically experienced many of the required pre-med courses, sometimes even before graduating from high school. College would be my first exposure to all of the pre-med courses. If I was not accepted into medical school, I told Phil, it would not be a devastating experience for me. After all, what I really wanted was to experience courses in math, physics and chemistry. These are subjects I had never expected to take in the not so distant past. However, since my arrival in America, I had evolved into a different person and I found myself intrigued with new interests. My life had taken a detour for the better and my interests no longer revolved around solely my social activities. I now wanted to pursue a new interest that would challenge my brain and I decided it might even be enjoyable to attend more college! I greatly admired my husband's brilliance and I was fortunate that he also encouraged me to challenge my own intellect.

I began my pre-med education at La Roche College, a small private college located next to North Hills Passavant Hospital. I arranged to work in the emergency department from 11am to 7pm. I took a general chemistry class in the morning before I began my 11 to 7 shift. The chemistry professor was Dr. Farrell and he seemed to appreciate my close attention to his instruction. I don't think he realized I was concerned I was in way over my head because I had never taken a similar class. He was supportive and kind to me and this was fortunate for me because I was still very insecure and I possessed a lack of self confidence. I worked hard and earned an 'A' in his class. Dr. Farrell spoke to me after he had graded the first test and told me the math I used to answer the problem for extra credit was not 'usual math' but that I had somehow arrived at the answer correct. I had to explain that I had not yet taken adequate math courses to answer this extra credit problem so I had to use math strategies I thought might work. I was taken aback when Dr. Farrell apologized to me at the end of his course that he could not present me with an award to recognize my accomplishment in his chemistry class. He told me he could only present awards to students actually enrolled in a degree program. I was truly honored by his comments and his comments alone were an award to me, albeit a private one. I considered my A in his course was a necessary grade if I had any hope of acceptance into medical school.

After I had completed two successful semesters in chemistry at La Roche College, I transferred to Slippery Rock University (by this time Slippery Rock State College had become Slippery Rock University). I took only pre-med science courses because I had already accumulated sixty credits from nursing school. The Slippery

Rock University professors, not unlike Dr. Farrell, were all very encouraging and they urged me to continue my quest, that is, all except for one teacher, the physics professor. After I took my first ever physics test I was devastated because I found the test difficult even though I felt I had prepared well for it. I was miserable when I saw my grade because it was a measly 75 percent! I decided to meet with the instructor to express my concern to him. I explained I was very upset because I had been doing so well in all of my courses up until now. Gaining admission into medical school was beginning to seem possible, that is, until I took his physics test. I told him that a mediocre physics grade would keep me from being accepted into medical school and I was looking for suggestions on how to perform better on the tests. I was shocked when the instructor nonchalantly and smugly replied, "Well, some people have it, and some people don't." Clearly, this was not the response I was expecting. I was used to receiving only encouraging words and kind support from my teachers. I was stunned and I felt angry upon experiencing his arrogance. I left his office without saying another word because I immediately concluded this imbecile was not worthy of my request for assistance.

Even though I had not performed well on my first physics test and the smug professor was very demoralizing, I knew I had not reached this point of my success to let the likes of this arrogant fool to be proven correct. I was not about to accept his assumption that I do not have 'it'. I decided a different strategy was in order in my approach as to how I learn physics. After I had completed the next physics test I felt much more confident about my performance as I handed it in to the physics professor. Still, I was not expecting to do as well as I did. When I was handed my corrected test during class, I was dumbfounded. I announced in disbelief to my classmate, who was seated at the desk in front of mine, "Wow, I got a 99 percent!" I did not realize he was holding a cup of coffee as I excitedly slapped him on his back. He unfortunately spilled his warm coffee all over his nice, freshly pressed shirt. He was a good sport about the incident and he smiled and told me it was okay. This very nice classmate was an engineering student and he too was a very good and serious student. He was always genuinely happy for me when I earned 98 percent or higher on every physics test thereafter, because he knew of my dismay when I received my initial test back and of the lack of encouragement I had received from Dr. Condescending at the beginning of the course.

Towards the end of the physics course, I took the opportunity to give the self-serving physics professor a piece of my mind. It was on a day when I was actually sitting alone with him in the physics classroom. He was seated on a desk at one end of the classroom, and I was seated on a desk at the other end of the classroom. I couldn't resist the temptation to remind him of his discouraging words to me when he had smugly told me that, "Some people have it and some people do not." The professor no longer looked smug, especially since I now possessed the highest grade in his class, higher than even his most prized engineering students! He appeared uncomfortable and embarrassed as I spoke to him and asked him to please remember his demoralizing words to me in his future associations with his 'bright eyed and bushy tailed' students when they come to him for some advice and support. I told him he was unsympathetic towards me and that he did not give me the support that a teacher should provide to a student who is requesting assistance. I reminded him that it is his responsibility to encourage his students and not to dispirit them, as he had done in my case. Fortunately, I was able to bounce back despite his demeaning words to me. I told him I was concerned because I believe his unkind and thoughtless words would be enough to cause many students to give up and drop out of college. It was my intention to make him realize how devastating his flippant and thoughtless words can be when he interacts with a student who is requesting his assistance and instead of mocking the student, perhaps he will encourage and assist the student appropriately in the future.

Chapter 17 – Oh My, How You Have Changed!

It wasn't long after the incident with the physics professor that I realized how much I had changed since my initial arrival from England. I was sitting and socializing with several college students over our lunch break. One topic of conversation was our grades, and I almost toppled off my seat in disbelief when one of my classmates commented to me that I couldn't possibly know what it is like to get less than an 'A' in one of my classes. I was left speechless and almost in shock. I sat quietly and pondered to myself that I had undergone a major transformation since my arrival here in the U.S. Adding to this, it was around this time that I received a letter from my friend Margaret, in England. She and I were in nursing school together before I came to the America. Margaret wrote in her letter to me that she was having trouble coming to terms with the fact that I was now studying to become a doctor. She wrote further that, no insult intended, I was the last person on earth she would have expected to become a doctor because I never studied and I always did the bare minimum I had to do to get by academically when I lived in England. I didn't take any offense at her comments because I knew she was stating a fact. Still, I was struck by the remarkable contrast being expressed to me by two friends at the same time. For example, I have a current classmate who thinks I have always been the top student of my classes and I therefore couldn't possibly know what it is like NOT to do well in my classes, and now I have received a letter from a former classmate in England who writes that she can't believe I actually do my homework and that I am now studying to become a doctor. I personally enjoyed the contrast because I anticipated that the experience of having been a participant on both sides of the fence in education would prove to be important at some time in my future. Indeed, to this day, I respect all people, no matter what level of education they have reached because, I am well aware there are brilliant people who have earned various educational degrees at higher institutions of learning, and likewise, there are brilliant people who have simply not had the opportunity or the interest to attend an educational institution beyond high school.

Things became quite hectic at one point during one of my semesters in college. I continued to work as an emergency room nurse and I was taking classes in physics, calculus and biology. I recall being fascinated to learn that one can calculate exactly where a ball will land on the ground as it rolls down off a sloped roof. Prior to these classes, I had thought the best one can do to estimate where a ball will land in a situation such as this is to simply guess, or to physically roll the ball down off the roof several times to determine if it lands in a reproducible fashion. This is exactly why I wanted to take classes in math and physics. I had wanted to learn details such as these because previously, I had never realized that one could mathematically precisely determine such ordinary daily measurements.

About half way through this semester, my cat, Lola, became very ill. She was vomiting and she became dehydrated. We took her to the vet and he rehydrated her by injecting her with copious amounts of fluid under her skin. I was relieved as she slowly recovered from her serious illness. During Lola's illness, I had a dream one night which combined a lot of these different themes. In my dream, I was taking an exam that involved both math and physics and one of the questions on the test involved a cat that was vomiting! Information that was provided on the test question was the speed of the vomit as it was ejected from the cat's mouth; and the trajectory that the vomited material took before it landed on some new carpet! The task of the test question was to calculate exactly where on the floor the vomited material landed. When I awoke from this dream the following morning I was amused as I realized I had combined the details of my sick cat with the subject material of my math and physics test! I also began to realize that perhaps I was in dire need of a vacation, perhaps hiking in the mountains where the air is fresh and crisp!

The time had come to take the medical college admission test, abbreviated the M.C.A.T. When my results arrived I was disappointed because some of the scores seemed to me to be only average, and I was therefore concerned that my results were not high enough to guarantee admission to medical school. I therefore decided to spruce up my knowledge base and so I took an M.C.A.T. prep course. I was thrilled when my test results increased from single digit to double digit values as a result of having taken this course, and I was now much more confident because I knew achievement of high scores on this test were a very important part of my application for entry into medical school. I was surprised later when I was told at one of my medical school interviews that it had not been necessary for me to repeat the M.C.A.T. because my first scores were adequate for acceptance into medical school. The interviewer had asked me why I had taken the test a second time and he joked in a kindly fashion that he knew it was not just for fun! I had applied for admission to both allopathic and osteopathic medical schools. After researching the different types of schools, I had learned that a student earns an M.D., or a 'medical doctor' degree at an allopathic school, whereas a student earns a D.O., or an 'osteopathic doctor' degree at an osteopathic school. As I read about the characteristics of the applicants to the various medical schools, I learned that the average M.C.A.T. score and G.P.A. of students accepted by the schools was lower at the osteopathic schools when compared to the allopathic schools. Phil and I had both completed our college education with a 4.0 G.P.A. Phil was happy because he was accepted by the first company that interviewed him, namely Sperry Corporation in Philadelphia. The company is currently known as Unisys Corporation. I therefore began to concentrate my efforts on applying to medical schools in Philadelphia. I, like Phil, was fortunate to be accepted by the first school that interviewed me, namely Jefferson Medical College. Phil and I were elated when I received my letter of acceptance in the mail because we now could move to Philadelphia, the city of brotherly love.

Chapter 18 – Goal Attained! On To Medical School

My coworkers in the emergency department were visibly shocked when I announced I had applied for admission to medical school and that I had been accepted and would be moving to Philadelphia to attend Jefferson Medical College. I was very happy and I had to periodically pinch myself to be sure I wasn't dreaming. As I expected, some nurses were very happy about my news while others expressed frank displeasure upon learning of my good fortune. I was disturbed when a sourpuss secretary in the emergency department complained bitterly, in my presence, about 'my situation' to one of her coworkers. She complained that 'foreigners' should not be allowed to come to this country and attend medical school because they do not pay taxes. I promptly corrected this ignorant and nasty individual and explained to her that I, a foreigner, have to pay taxes, just as she has to pay taxes. I explained to her further that I, however, am not permitted to vote even though I pay taxes (at the time I was not a U.S. citizen). I told her that in future, she should have an adequate knowledge base before she makes such mean-spirited accusations. At this, she was quiet. I don't think she expected me to defend myself so vehemently. I was very annoyed at her idiocy. She did not complain after this, at least, not in my presence. I suspect however that she voiced a multitude of racist remarks in my absence because that is simply the type of person she was and nothing I said was going to change that fact.

Before I had decided upon Jefferson Medical College as the medical school I wanted to attend, I had traveled to St. Louis, Missouri to interview at Washington University Medical School. Phil and I shared the drive and my mother accompanied us for the ride. This entire trip was a disaster and in hindsight I would have been better off if I had not gone for the interview. During our drive to Missouri there was a major icy blizzard and the highway was sheer ice. Many trucks speeded past us on the highway and then predictably, one or two miles later, we saw these same trucks overturned on the highway! This was truly a white-knuckle driving experience for all three of us. The interstate highway was literally closing behind us as we drove forward at a turtle's pace of 20 M.P.H. Fortunately, we arrived in St. Louis safely, but this horrendous travel experience turned out to be strike number one of three strikes against this medical school. On the day of my interview a medical student gave interviewees a tour of the medical school grounds. This medical student expressed extreme dissatisfaction with the school. He told us that the medical school faculty makes it apparent to the students that a career in research is preferred and it discourages medical students from choosing a career in primary care medicine. This medical student complained that he would have chosen a different medical school if he had known of this negative attitude towards primary care medicine because he was choosing to be a clinician and not a researcher. This was strike number two against the school because I too was favoring a career in clinical medicine rather than research. My interview was strike number three against the school. The interviewer reminded me of Ben Stiller, both in appearance and personality, when he appeared as the obnoxious gym leader in the hit movie, Dodge Ball. He also clearly suffered from the Napoleon complex. He behaved in an egotistic manner from the very start of the interview, and when he became aware that I was Registered Nurse, he became outright arrogant. He scoffed as he read my qualifications written on my application and he expressed his patronizing opinion to me that too many nurses are becoming physicians and that this is not acceptable. I found his comments to be surprising since all physicians I had encountered up until now had informed me that they considered my career in nursing to be a great asset and not a detriment, for my career switch to a physician. I formally complained to the administration officials of the medical school about my interviewer's pompous remarks and obnoxious attitude towards me. The administrative officials expressed great concern about my appalling experience and I was offered an interview with a different doctor. By now, however, the damage was irreparable and I told the officials of the school that I was no longer interested in attending this medical school. I did, however, ask that the school investigate the attitude of my interviewer further, because his behavior indicated he had a personal vendetta against nurse applicants.

68

I went on to interview at Hahnemann Medical School. I wasn't nervous despite a mix up at my interview, most likely because I already had my acceptance at Jefferson. The person who was supposed to interview me was out of the country and so another physician was called to interview me. He was very candid and asked me what other medical schools I had applied to, and he also asked if I had received any acceptances as of yet. His reaction surprised me when I explained I had been accepted by Jefferson. He exclaimed, "Why on earth are you interviewing here if you have been accepted at Jefferson?" I told him I was enjoying the interview process and that I wanted to evaluate the schools for myself and not simply accept a standardized rating system of the schools that was available in books. As I left Hahnemann school that day I left with a negative impression. It wasn't the interview that I thought badly of because I had appreciated the frankness and honesty of my interviewer. I had a negative impression because I saw many medical students leaving the auditorium at break time and rushing to immediately light up their cigarettes. It was at times like this that I realized how deeply the untimely death of my father due to his cigarette smoking had influenced me, because here it would play a role in the medical school I would ultimately choose to attend because of my attention to such details at my interviews.

I found it interesting and surprising that I chose to attend Jefferson Medical College because it was the last medical college to accept female applicants, and I decided against attending The Medical College of Pennsylvania, which was the first medical school to accept female applicants. The director of admissions at the Medical College of Pennsylvania was extremely encouraging towards me and she even called me while I was at work in the emergency department at Passavant Hospital to congratulate me that I had been accepted by her medical school. I remember I was extremely embarrassed at the time because I was attracted to Jefferson's medical school because of the more youthful and energetic campus when compared to the less appealing campuses of other medical schools. At this time, I found the issue of schools that promote female acceptance in the professional world to be less important. My face was flushed with embarrassment as I declined this attractive offer of acceptance from the medical director of the school who called me personally while I was at work. There was a shocked look of disbelief on each of the faces of my nurse colleagues as they witnessed my decline of this offer of acceptance. My colleagues were already aware I had acceptances elsewhere and I'm sure, just like me, they did not expect me to receive more than one acceptance by a medical school. I had crossed all the dots in my preparation for medical school so that if I was not accepted, it would not have been due to my lack of effort. Now it was obvious that my diligence and hard work was fruitful as evidenced by multiple acceptances.

Phil and I moved to Philadelphia in August 1985 and he began to work for Unisys Corporation. We stayed at a hotel for the first month in Plymouth Meeting because we couldn't move into the medical school housing until I matriculated in September. It was a wonderful month for me. I walked up and down Plymouth Meeting mall and I exercised daily at the fitness center. I remember the agony of my muscle aches which lasted a full week after my first aerobics class. I had never experienced such pain prior to this and I realized, in hindsight, that I should not have pushed my endurance so far during my first class. However, I had not been willing to accept defeat and in so doing appear less able than the other more seasoned participants in the class. I forced myself to continue the exercises, even though I was clearly in a class that was far too advanced for my level. It was a full week before I could move comfortably enough to resume exercise classes again! I was careful to go easier on myself this time and to gradually build on my flexibility and strength because I wanted to exercise daily and not weekly! August was a full month of contentment for me. I had no work schedule and no homework. We ate at various restaurants every day. I didn't even have to clean because the room was cleaned by the hotel cleaning staff. I was truly relaxed and blissful. I had succeeded in my goal to be accepted into medical school despite the tremendous odds that were stacked against me. I was rewarded with this full month in which I had no work requirements or school studies, and I was enjoying every minute of it!

My month of sheer bliss came to an end when it was time for Phil and me to move into Orlowitz, one of the Jefferson University campus student residence buildings. The building has twenty-four hour security which was reassuring; however our apartment was very small. Phil enjoyed the hustle and bustle of center-city life, whereas I found life in the city to be extremely unappealing and I longed for the beautiful foliage and more relaxed pace of the suburbs. There was another reason for my distaste for the city. We lived in the city at a time when the courts ruled that many individuals with serious mental illnesses who had been housed in long term care facilities for many years were released to the streets. It was quickly apparent that many of these individuals were not able to fend for themselves. They were unable to be productive members of society because many of them suffered with severe psychotic mental illnesses and their thought patterns were not based on reality. A great number of them simply became homeless and they begged for money for their sustenance on the sidewalks of center city. I remember one individual would bang with a heavy hammer on the sidewalk constantly while talking to himself. I would pass him quickly and simply hope he would not suddenly swing out at me with the hammer because it was obvious his thoughts were not rational thoughts. It is often difficult for me to understand the rationale behind the work of the ACLU. Why did they work so hard to have these individuals released from a place where they were safe and taken care of, only to have them released on to the street without food, water, clothing or compassion? Another particularly unpleasant experience I came across was on one particular day, as I walked with my friend along Chestnut Street. A homeless man beckoned for our attention as he stood at the end of an alley. His pants were down and he was scruffy. He was masturbating feverishly and he expressed a 'dirty old man' toothless grin. As we stepped up onto the sidewalk on the other side of the road, another disheveled and toothless homeless man grinned at us and held out his soiled hand. He announced there was a charge of one quarter for the show! I am sure the mayor of the city would be proud that these two entrepreneurs were providing reasonably priced entertainment for visitors to the city of brotherly love! Personally, I was looking forward to being able to leave Philadelphia to move into the suburbs, just as soon as it was practical to do so, given all of the brotherly love I had witnessed so far!

My classes in medical school were straightforward and we had exams one week of each month to make sure we were keeping up and studying the material. I preferred this approach over other medical schools which gave exams on a regular weekly basis because in those schools there is never a break from exams. Another way to explain this is to say I preferred a larger amount of academic pressure once each month over a smaller amount of academic pressure once a week! I enjoyed the high spirited energy of my medical school. I was one of the older, more mature students in my class who had the experience of a former career. Most of my classmates had straight-arrowed it from high school to pre-med and then they were accepted directly into medical school. In my classes, I had several memorable disagreements during group discussions with classmates who apparently thought quite differently about particular situations than I did. I was sometimes taken aback at how inexperienced some of my classmates were when they expressed the ways in which they would handle difficult medical situations that potentially could arise. On one occasion, I argued poignantly back and forth with a particular classmate who possessed a very different view from mine. It was after the heated arguments that I would feel bewildered and I would wonder how on earth an innocent discussion had deteriorated into a heated argument. On one occasion my close friend and I fell into this 'discussion becomes an argument' trap. It was on a day when a physician lecturer spoke in the auditorium on the thought provoking subject of teenage pregnancies. At the time I had no idea that my friend was a devout disciple of the right-to-life movement. I expressed my opinion to her, not realizing she would take great offense at my words, because I honestly expected any reasonable and logical person to share my opinion. I told her that in the case of a teenage pregnancy, I believe it is appropriate to consider each situation on an individual basis. Needless to say, I unintentionally offended my friend greatly, and we found ourselves in a heated discussion about abortion. This is obviously an issue that she cares passionately about and she argued with me that she believes there is absolutely no situation that exists in which abortion is appropriate. This argument sadly resulted in the diminution of our friendship. Immediately after our disagreement, she became cool and distant towards me and I was unable to rekindle the warmth of our former friendship. It became clear to me that she was unforgiving of our difference of opinion. If I had been aware of my friend's sharply differing viewpoint on this subject compared to my own, I would certainly have kept my opinion to myself. Thank goodness our spouses do not behave in a similar fashion! I am grateful to have a spouse who loves me unconditionally and who will be my friend forever, not only when we are in agreement, but also, after we have a disagreement. He has been a great support for me throughout our multiple decades of marriage and I believe he is the single greatest source of my academic success, my excellent mental health and also my physical wellbeing.

Chapter 19 – Tick Tock

In my third year of medical school I began to hear the tick-tock of my biological clock. Prior to this, Phil and I had been equally disinterested in becoming parents, but now my interest was changing. As Phil and I strolled along our favorite walking trail outside of Chestnut Hill, I cautiously approached him about my changing interest and I went on to say, "I know we both agreed we would be happy together without children, but now I am thinking it might be nice to have a child after all." It was a surprise to me that Phil was instantly agreeable and he told me this would also be of interest to him. For the first time after ten years of marriage, we were planning a family! This was quite a contrast compared to our prior activities in which we were extremely careful to prevent pregnancy. Concurrently, my interest in a certain line of clothing developed as I took notice of fashionable items in the maternity stores and I also eyed the cute baby clothing stores. I was excited about becoming pregnant and I did not expect to have any difficulties with my fertility since none were present in any members of my family. I was both surprised and disappointed when I realized that, unlike all my siblings, I did not simply blink and become pregnant! The first month passed and then the second month and then even the third month, the pregnancy tests were always negative! I bought an ovulation detector kit which turned the correct color and this therefore confirmed I was at least ovulating. Additionally, there was no celebration of a pregnancy for me during months four, five and six. I scheduled an appointment with an infertility specialist. Phil was evaluated and his little sperm creatures were found to be alive and well and they possessed a good sense of direction. I was scheduled to have an endometrial biopsy and I graciously gave permission for his conscientious medical resident to perform the procedure. I was assured that this procedure is a 'piece of cake' and that it is not painful. I was not at all concerned or anxious about the procedure since this used to be performed every three months many years ago on patients who were prescribed estrogen replacement therapy. As I underwent the procedure, the medical resident followed the usual technique to create a vacuum to draw the sample from the endometrial lining of my womb into the tube. As she created the vacuum, I unexpectedly experienced gut-wrenching waves of cramps originating from my womb which then spread like nauseating tentacles throughout my entire body. Immediately thereafter, I felt as if I was in the oppressive and suffocating humidity of the rain forest and I became drenched in sweat and then promptly lost consciousness. The next thing I remember was the awful pungent ammonia odor of smelling salts and I quickly opened my eyes to witness the concerned faces of the doctor and his resident physician as they gently held my hands. As an explanation for what had occurred, the doctor insisted I must have been anxious and this is why I passed out. However, I knew that anxiety does not cause the intense pain I had experienced. I concluded that the endometrial biopsy probe withdrew material too deeply from the lining of my womb and this resulted in stimulation of the autonomic nervous system throughout my body. In turn, the stimulation of this portion of the nervous system caused my blood pressure and pulse to plummet, and this rendered me unconscious. I also knew it was possible that the complication may have been the result of the inexperience of the resident physician. This procedure had been unexpectedly difficult and I preferred not to have it repeated at any time in the future.

Happily, all of our infertility testing was normal. However, as the end of my fourth year of medical school approached, I still was not pregnant. After much thought and consideration, I told the doctor I would halt my pregnancy plans until my internship year of residency was completed, because I was concerned I could potentially be a burden to my fellow residents. I therefore planned to resume my efforts to become pregnant once I was in the second year of my residency. After the first year of residency my call schedule would not intertwine so closely with that of my fellow residents. I considered my decision in this matter to be logical and rationale since I had personally witnessed many instances where, indeed, the unexpected complications during pregnancy of an intern had leaned very heavily on the other interns. The last thing I wanted was to be a burden to anyone. I was completely taken aback when the doctor expressed extreme anger at my decision to temporarily halt pregnancy attempts and I was then completely astounded when he actually slammed the wall with his hand and insisted I should not interfere with my pregnancy efforts! One of my own, closely held values is that a doctor should not be influenced by his or her own personal beliefs such that they interfere with objectivity in the medical care of patients. It was now painfully apparent to me that my doctor did not share in my view because he expressed this inappropriate anger at my decision. By the end of my appointment I was relieved to quickly exit from his office. I decided I must obtain a new infertility specialist elsewhere when I resumed my attempts to become pregnant.

Chapter 20 – Turn off the Clock

When I was a medical student in my fourth year of medical school at Jefferson Hospital, I experienced some difficulty with an internal medicine intern who was responsible for my supervision. I had obtained the results of a blood count belonging to a hospitalized patient with cancer who was receiving chemotherapy. The patient's blood count was very low but I was not concerned because I concluded it was low because of the toxic effects of the chemotherapy. I therefore did not give the results of the blood count to my supervising intern until our group meeting at the end of the day. When I made him aware of the low blood count he became frantic and he reprimanded me in front of my team members for not reporting the results to him immediately after I had received them. I was surprised at his reaction because his demeanor was usually dull but calm. Despite my explanation to him that the blood count was expectedly low because of the patient's chemotherapy, he insisted that I accompany him to the cancer patient's room to obtain a stat blood count. The unfortunate patient possessed scarred veins due to the multiplicity of prior blood draws and she cried out in pain as he repeatedly stabbed needles into the veins of her feet to try to obtain a small sample of blood for the repeat test. He had to get blood from her foot because she had no suitable remaining access for blood on her arms and hands due to scarring. The next morning, the patient's cancer specialist was furious when his patient bitterly complained to him about the awful and painful blood drawing experience she had endured the night before. The cancer specialist scolded the intern and explained to him that, just as I had told him, the blood count was expectedly low because of the chemotherapy! The intern was very humiliated by his obvious medical ignorance and the cancer specialist insisted appropriately that the intern apologize to his patient for subjecting her to the unnecessary suffering. I did not receive an apology from this intern for humiliating me inappropriately in front of my fellow classmates but then I did not expect to receive one either.

As one can summarize from the experience above, my prior clinical experience as a registered nurse was immensely helpful to me during my clinical rotations in the hospitals. This is because I was already familiar with most medical situations that I encountered and I was comfortable managing the clinical situations independently of others. I was fortunate that the phrase which is well known to medical residents, 'Watch one procedure, then do that procedure, and then teach the procedure' usually did not pertain to me because I had an abundance of practical experience to draw from due to my experience as an emergency room nurse before I entered medical school. A typical example would be the dreaded medical resident task of starting intravenous lines. This is usually very stressful for most student doctors because he or she is called to the patient's bedside to start an intravenous line only after the most experienced nurse from the intravenous team has been unable to start the line. Picture the scene; an inexperienced student doctor is called to start an intravenous line on a patient for whom the expert nurse from the intravenous team has failed at accomplishing the task. The anxious student doctor's hands typically shake so uncontrollably due to nervousness and this only makes matters worse! I was grateful that I never found myself in this embarrassing and humbling predicament because I had started many intravenous lines during my years as an emergency department nurse. There were countless occasions in medical school and then later in my residency that I greatly appreciated numerous clinical skills I had learned as a nurse

I graduated from medical school and, interestingly, like me, many of my friends who were also highly ranked in the class chose to become family doctors. It surprised me that such a high percentage of the top students in my class chose family medicine as their specialty because, rumor has it, that less highly ranked students choose this field of medicine because it is not a financially rewarding field in medicine. In other words, it is a common assumption that the residency positions in the more lucrative fields of medicine are only offered to the more competitive and more highly ranked students. Interestingly, I was surprised to find that in my class, class rank did not correlate with the choice of medical specialty. I personally chose to specialize in family medicine because I wanted to avoid boredom in my life and I therefore sought challenge by constant exposure to the many different areas of medicine. Some of the specialties I was exposed to in medical school had a very narrow spectrum of expertise and I quickly became bored; I knew this would be a problem for me because I wanted an intellectually challenging career. Thankfully, medical students are a diverse group and have different interests and preferences for specific areas in medicine. It is important that each field of medicine maintains an adequate supply of doctors. We would be in a sorry state of affairs if we all chose the same medical specialty!

When I entered medical school I expected that I would become either an emergency physician or a cardiologist. My interests changed when I was exposed to the dynamic faculty of Jefferson's Department of Family Medicine. I had not been aware of the existence of a specialty called family medicine prior to my matriculation into medical school and I was excited to learn of it. Why did this specialty attract me so much? I found it was the lure of being positioned such that I could have a positive influence on the longevity and wellness of my patients. The emphasis of family medicine is on prevention, such as encouraging a patient to stop smoking, and controlling a patient's cholesterol and blood pressure. The impact of this intervention could then potentially prevent a heart attack or a stroke, ten or even twenty years later. I wanted to be positioned such that I could benefit my patients' lives by applying my tenacious interest in promoting and maintaining their wellness, and I knew I would be satisfied and fulfilled if I could do this for them. Because I was drawn to the philosophy of prevention, I concluded my skills would be constantly challenged if I became a family medicine doctor. It was, however, made clear to me that not everybody was as excited about the field of family medicine as I was. For example, one of my classmates told me that he did not understand my interest in family medicine. In fact, he specifically asked me why I wanted to be, 'jack of all trades and master of none'. On the other hand, I likewise, was critical of him because he chose neurosurgery as his specialty even though he suffered with chronic back problems. I envisioned him as a neurosurgeon in a few short years with daily misery due to worsening back pain because of prolonged hours stooped over the operating room table. I wondered why on earth he would choose a field of medicine in which the stress on his back would likely cause progressive and worsening back pain. I concluded that he must hold such high regard for his own personal sense of prestige and therefore the particular specialty he would choose. The prestigious specialty of neurosurgery was clearly more attractive to him than any concern he might have about the future misery of back pain.

I applied to several Family Medicine residency programs. I had spent some time as a medical student at the family medicine residency program at Chestnut Hill Hospital. I was attracted to this program because, unlike most residency programs, the upper year resident physicians did not supervise the newer resident physicians; instead the attending physicians supervised the resident physicians. Most of my fellow classmates did not choose this residency program because they actually wanted close, round-the -clock supervision by the upper year resident physicians. My situation was different because, unlike most of my classmates, I had my prior clinical experience as an emergency room nurse. I knew this experience would be invaluable to help manage the various medical emergencies which typically arise overnight, when only the resident physicians are present in the hospital and their attending physicians are in their homes, and therefore unavailable for an immediate response. I was confident I could handle the various medical emergent situations that were likely to arise, and I actually preferred to manage the situations on my own rather than to have my medical decisions restricted by an upper year resident physician.

Phil and I were also interested in moving to Florida and so I applied to two residency programs in Florida, one in St. Petersburg and one in Orlando. I decided to spend one week at each program so that I could carefully evaluate each one. I first went to the residency program in Orlando which I found out was associated with the Seventh Day Adventist church. Phil and I were invited out to dinner with one of the residents and his wife to discuss the program. It was soon apparent to me that I would not be comfortable at this highly religious program. For example, the resident told me they group together and pray over patients each morning during their morning rounds. I knew I would be very uncomfortable with this arrangement because I would be inpatient and anxious to start looking up lab results and test results for my patients to help with their diagnoses so that the patient would be able to return home as soon as possible. Next, I was concerned to learn that this religion permits no consumption of caffeine or meat and this information did not sit well with me! Phil and I both concluded I was not compatible with this program because I am agnostic and also because I thoroughly enjoy both coffee and meat. The next morning I gracefully declined my interview with the director of the residency program. The medical secretary was clearly disturbed by my decision and she begged me, "Please do not leave until you meet with the director so he can see that you are not a heathen!" Her words of concern only served to underscore further the appropriateness of my decision to bow out and I swiftly moved on to the next residency program in St. Petersburg without meeting the program director!

The residency program in St. Petersburg was much more to my liking. I did spend over a week at this program but I concluded my experience with two concerns. One was my personal distaste for the typical supervision of first year residents by upper year residents. I preferred to be supervised by doctors that had more clinical experience than the residents simply because I already possessed more clinical experience than many of the residents because of my years of work as an emergency room nurse. The second concern I developed was triggered on an occasion when I entered the resident lounge and came across only male residents sitting at a table, playing cards together. I was immediately uncomfortable because the residents appeared to frown as they looked over at me, signifying to me that I was trespassing on their male turf. There was not a single female resident present and I was saddened to sense a male chauvinistic atmosphere. My concern was validated the next day by a female intern within the residency program. She had been very enthusiastic about the residency program during my initial correspondence with her when she first entered the program. Now I was witnessing a great deal of dissatisfaction and frustration as she described the unfairness she was experiencing. She had initially been vibrant and animated but now, in stark contrast, she appeared haggard, distraught and lonely. I decided there was too much potential in this residency program for an abuse of power which potentially could make my residency experience miserable. I was not afraid of long hours and hard work but I knew from experience I would be intolerant of blatant unfairness simply because of my gender. When I returned to Chestnut Hill, Philadelphia, after just two weeks in Florida, I was captivated by the beauty and the culture of Chestnut Hill. Florida no longer held any appeal to me and I greatly appreciated the presence of an expectation of equality between men and women which existed in Pennsylvania, an expectation of equality which I unfortunately had found to be lacking in Florida. I was now aware that for me, this sense of equality was crucial, and I would no longer take its presence for granted. I ranked the Chestnut Hill Family Medicine residency program first on my application. I knew this program was not the first choice for many applicants because the majority of medical students, unlike me, were desirous of more upper year resident supervision than the Chestnut Hill program had to offer. I was very happy when I was one of the fortunate medical students that matched with their first choice on match day. I was told by my friend at the residency program in Saint Petersburg that their program had performed poorly in the match. I was surprised to hear this news because a majority of the residents in her program had expressed an expectation that their program was in high demand among applicants. Most likely, I was not the only applicant to detect an arrogant and chauvinistic attitude among the male residents and I suspected that this explained a poor match day for their program.

Chapter 21 – Medical Residency Begins

Before the start of my residency, Phil and I bought a small Cape Cod house in Oreland which is just outside of Chestnut Hill and only a five minute drive for me to get to the hospital for work. Our intent was to sell the house at the end of my residency once I knew where my permanent work as a family doctor would be. We decided this would serve as an investment for us in place of renting an apartment for three years and having nothing to show for it at the end of my residency.

On the first day of my residency experience I was surprised that most of my resident colleagues had fearful and white, pasty faces. The hospital's teaching attending physicians advised us of our responsibilities as they assigned us to the overnight call schedule. We were told each of us would be on call overnight in the hospital every fourth night. On our call nights, we would work a full day, continue working overnight, and then finish up with another full day of work. This accounted for a total of twenty eight hours work in the hospital without going home, and often without any sleep! My first night on call was hellish experience! There was an onslaught of patients that required hospital admission and we divided the work among the available residents in as fair a manner as possible. At one point I took a few moments to lie down on my bed because I was both mentally and physically exhausted. As I lay on my back, the room seemed to spin, around and around. I was distraught that my first night on call had turned out to be such a harrowing experience. Mine had not been one of the pale and pasty faces that I had seen at the beginning of the day because I was quite confident I could handle almost any medical situation. But now, I too had a pale and pasty face. I was no longer confident that I could tolerate additional call nights, especially if they were going to be as torturous as this night. As I lay on my bed feeling very discouraged, my pager went off. A temporary agency nurse in the coronary care unit notified me of a change in the status of a patient who had complained of chest pain over the past forty five minutes. Unfortunately, the nurse had wasted precious time by repeating several EKG's before she had contacted me to come to evaluate the patient. As I assessed the patient, it was clear he was experiencing a heart attack and valuable time had been wasted by the nurse before she had called me to the patient. I rendered emergency care to the patient while his cardiologist was urgently called in to the hospital. He was understandably livid about the delay in his patient's care and I was disturbed when the nurse was not truthful about the reason for the delay and she instead attempted to pin the blame on me. Fortunately, each of the EKG's the nurse had performed before she had contacted me had the time printed on the EKG paper. I was relieved to be vindicated because it was clear by assessing the sequence of events that I was the truthful person. When the supervisor of nursing arrived at work that morning, she apologized profusely to me and she immediately fired the nurse. She was clearly embarrassed by her nurse's dishonest and unprofessional behavior. I was greatly relieved when my torturous first night on call came to an end. Although I experienced subsequent challenging call nights, they all paled in comparison to this nerve-racking first night on call experience.

Later in the year, I was rounding on my assigned patients in the hospital, at the beginning of my call night. A teenage black male was in a room on his own on the regular medical floor. I was concerned because he did not respond to me when I smiled at him and said hello. The nurses were scarce and they were busily tending to other patients. I quickly looked over his chart and determined that he was receiving an intravenous infusion containing morphine to control his pain due to sickle cell disease. I concluded he was in respiratory failure caused by the intravenous morphine and the patient's attending doctor had demonstrated a lack of good judgment by leaving this patient in such a precarious situation. I did not call the patient's doctor because I knew what needed to be done for this young man and I did not want any interference with my decision making. I turned off the morphine infusion and I checked the patient's oxygen level which was critically low. I immediately had him transferred to the intensive care unit so that he could be continuously closely monitored by the nurses. I also contacted the chief respiratory therapist and he shared my concern about this critically ill teenager. The respiratory therapist stayed at the patient's bedside to continuously assess his respiratory status and he informed me that the patient's breathing continued to decline despite our best efforts to maintain his oxygen level. We had no choice but to intubate the young patient and assist his breathing through a respirator because he was losing the battle of his life. We continued to closely monitor the young man for the remainder of the night and he fortunately stabilized on the respirator. I did not call the chief pulmonologist until the following morning because I knew there was nothing additional that he would do. I advised the pulmonologist of the situation by phone and he was clearly pleased with my management of the situation. He told me he would be in to assess the patient after he had his breakfast and morning shower since the patient was now stable. Both the pulmonologist and the patient's attending physician arrived to see the patient at about the same time, and I was disturbed to overhear the patient's attending physician apologize to the specialist that I had not called him in to the hospital sooner. The patient's doctor went on to complain that he was perturbed because he had not been notified by me of his patient's critical condition until that morning either. I was surprised when the pulmonary specialist told the patient's doctor that I had acted responsibly in taking care of his patient and that the patient had been given competent and excellent care by me. The patient's doctor then agreed that my care had been appropriate and he said no more of the situation. Later, as I stood by the patient's bed he was now wide awake and alert. He held out his arms and then he hugged me tightly and spoke loudly, "Thank you for saving my life!" I looked at his face and saw he had a handsome broad smile. It occurred to me that even though he had been unconscious throughout most of the night, he had been more aware of the events that had unfolded than I had realized. I continued my work that day feeling very tired but gratified that I had been responsible for saving this young man's life.

On another memorable night in the hospital that year, I was called to the room of a middle aged male patient who, the nurse told me, was having difficulty breathing. When I entered the patient's room I was immediately concerned because he was alert but it was clear to me he was suffering greatly. He was pleasant and friendly despite his serious condition and he was breathless as he attempted to answer my questions. Brown, coffee ground material, which is old blood, was pooling inside his mouth and it flowed from the corners of his mouth as he spoke. I knew his stomach was distended with old blood, much like when a balloon is distended with fluid, and that is why it leaked from his mouth. I acted promptly to relieve his distress by placing a stomach tube gently through his nose into his stomach. I then attached a large syringe to the end of the tube and drew up the brown coffee ground liquid from his stomach over and over to fill the syringe, each time emptying the contents of the syringe into a large bucket. Once the pressure due to the high volume of old blood in his stomach was relieved he was able to breathe more comfortably and speak to me without blood trickling out from the corners of his mouth. He grimaced because he had severe pain and his sister, a nun, begged me to relieve his pain. All of the usual analgesics to relieve pain had been administered but they had not been effective. I knew that a morphine intravenous infusion was necessary to relieve this man's pain but I also knew the morphine would suppress his respirations and he could potentially die. I explained this problem to the patient and his sister, but they still requested that I give the morphine anyhow, his sister citing that her brother had already suffered enough. I contacted the patient's oncologist and spoke with him on the phone. The oncologist did not want his patient to receive morphine because this would mean that the oncologist would have to come into the hospital from home to transfer his patient to the intensive care unit where he could be monitored for respiratory depression due to the morphine. As a resident, I was not permitted to order morphine in the intensive care unit without the supervision of the oncologist. The oncologist told me his patient should not be given the morphine on the regular hospital floor because his patient had a small chance that he could potentially survive this critical stage of his cancer. I was stuck uncomfortably in the middle, between the wishes of the patient and his sister, who wanted the morphine given for pain relief, and the orders of the oncologist, who said no morphine was to be given on the regular hospital floor but he was unwilling to come into the hospital to transfer his patient to the intensive care unit where the morphine could be given.

On this long, arduous night, this patient was suffering greatly due to pain and he and his sister continued to beg for my mercy. I had a difficult decision to make and I treated the situation as I would if it involved my own family member. I cleared my head and I decided I should explain to the patient my dilemma and then ask this man what his wishes are. The patient was clear in his desire and he requested that I relieve his intense pain by giving him the morphine. I informed the oncologist that his patient had requested morphine for his pain and that I would administer it because, as a resident, I could administer morphine on a regular hospital floor. The oncologist expressed his dissatisfaction with my decision but I explained he had left me with two difficult choices; leave his patient in excruciating pain or administer the morphine to give him relief. I explained I had chosen to follow the wishes of the patient and his sister by relieving his pain. I checked in on the patient shortly after beginning the morphine infusion and he no longer grimaced in pain. He now appeared relaxed and peaceful as he drifted into a much needed rest. The night was long but rewarding because I knew I had rescued this poor man, and his sister, from their unnecessary misery. The patient did die that night. I knew this would probably have been the outcome even if he had been transferred to the intensive care unit because the coffee ground stomach contents were a sign of serious internal bleeding. I greatly appreciated a beautifully written personal note the next day from the nun thanking me profusely for my compassion in the care of her brother and for allowing him to die with dignity.

Another situation in which an attending physician did not agree with my decision making was during an emergency room experience and I remember the scenario well. I was called at about four o' clock in the morning to assess a middle aged female patient who presented to the hospital with shortness of breath and she was coughing up bloody material. She was sitting upright on the emergency room stretcher in a room close to the nurses' station so she could be monitored closely. I asked her to produce sputum so I could examine it and she complied with my request and coughed material up into a tissue. The material was like frothy saliva containing a copious amount of bright red blood. Her EKG and blood work results were normal except for her arterial blood gases which showed a low oxygen level. Her chest x-ray was stunning because it was white, indicating her lungs were filled with fluid, instead of the normal black appearance of lungs which are filled with air. This clinical picture usually indicates congestive heart failure, but I suspected instead that this patient had a respiratory problem and not a cardiac problem. I made this conclusion because the patient's secretions appeared to be frank blood and not the usual pink frothy fluid that one expects to see when a patient has congestive heart failure. I concluded also that the lungs were filled with frank blood and this was the cause of the white appearance on the chest x-ray. I decided to consult Dr. Hotair, the pulmonologist that was on call, rather than the cardiologist, because I believed this was a respiratory issue rather than a cardiac issue. Dr. Hotair was not happy and he stormed in to the emergency department like an angry bear. He was upset that I had called him in to the hospital in the early morning hours to see this patient. I had called Dr. Hotair because I had concluded the patient needed a pulmonary procedure called a bronchoscopy to assess the source of her bleeding. Dr. Hotair disagreed with my assessment and he complained bitterly to my family medicine supervisor, Dr. Barbara Coppa. He told Dr. Coppa that this was an obvious case of congestive heart failure and that the cardiologist should have been called in to the hospital and not him. He complained further to Dr. Coppa that she should supervise my diagnostic skills more closely so that I do not call the wrong specialist again in the future at such an inconvenient hour. I was shocked at his intolerance of my decision and by his obnoxious attitude as he chastised me openly in front of the hospital staff. I later came across Dr. Hotair in the hospital cafeteria. He continued to complain openly and loudly to all the attending physicians that I had awakened him and called him in to the hospital inappropriately and that I should have known it was a typical case for the cardiologist. I was disturbed by his arrogant and pompous attitude and I was still confident that I was correct in my diagnosis. Dr. Coppa came to speak to me later before I started my patient hours in the family medicine clinic. She spoke kindly to me and she reassured me that it was expected I would make mistakes such as these because I was still in my training. I did not defend my decision making to her because it was clear she also was convinced it was a typical case of heart failure and not the unexpected and unusual presentation of the condition I had diagnosed. Later that same morning, Dr. Coppa came to me and she told me she had to eat a large piece of humble pie. She told me that Dr. Blicker, a young and bright cardiologist, had been called in by Dr. Hotair to treat my patient for congestive heart failure. However, Dr. Blicker disagreed with Dr. Hotair's assessment and he diagnosed a pulmonary cause for her condition, not a cardiac cause. Dr. Blicker wrote in his report on the patient's chart that he agreed with my assessment, that this lady had a pulmonary problem and not a cardiac problem. He called Dr. Hotair back onto the case to perform a bronchoscopy, the procedure I had originally recommended! I was vindicated because Dr. Hotair had to visualize for himself through his bronchoscope that the patient's major airway was hemorrhaging due to severe tracheitis, just as I had suspected! On the contrary, the patient's heart was healthy and strong and therefore it was not susceptible to congestive heart failure. As I had concluded, it was pure blood in her lungs which was seen as 'white' on her chest x-ray, and not fluid due to congestive heart failure. Such joy is rare for a resident to experience. My arrogant and abhorrent teacher was seen for what he was, a total jackass. He had complained bitterly to all the hospital physicians that my judgment was in error and his was correct. Now he had to acknowledge that he, a Pulmonologist, had misdiagnosed a pulmonary condition as a cardiac ailment, even though a mere resident physician had already correctly diagnosed the condition for him! Dr. Blicker seemed outwardly gleeful that I had demonstrated superior diagnostic skills over Dr. Hotair even in his own specialty! I expect the other attending physicians told Dr. Blicker how badly Dr. Hotair had treated me. Dr. Hotair never did apologize to me, unlike Dr. Coppa, who sincerely apologized for her assumption that my diagnosis was incorrect. I know she was embarrassed by the situation and she had been disturbed that Dr. Hotair had publicly ridiculed me. It is because Dr. Hotair was such an insensitive imbecile that I write this experience truthfully and without softening the blow to him. If he had apologized and treated me in a dignified manner and with respect, I would be more cognizant of his feelings at this time. As it is however, I now show Dr. Hotair the same lack of respect that he showed me when he disagreed with my diagnosis. It is a satisfying experience when the good 'David' is able to topple the mean spirited 'Goliath'.

Chapter 22 – Dr. Inept

One of my pediatric rotations took place in the second year of my residency program and it turned out to be a disappointing, albeit interesting, experience. I trained at Abington Memorial Hospital and my direct supervisor was Dr. Peggy Inept. She was employed by the hospital and her duties included teaching, supervising and evaluating family medicine residents during the pediatric rotation at the hospital. Dr. Inept was pregnant during my rotation and it so happened that I had resumed infertility evaluation and treatments during this rotation. The appointments for my infertility care blended in nicely with my work on the pediatric unit without problems because my new infertility specialist, Dr. Jay Schinfeld, was a staff member at the same hospital.

I found it disturbing that Dr. Inept demonstrated a lack of respect for nurses and she would regularly speak in a condescending manner to residents about the nurses. I do not believe the nurses were aware of this because Dr. Inept spoke with a quiet voice and her demeaning comments were usually expressed outside of their hearing range or in a separate room. Dr. Inept's inconsiderate attitude bothered me because I found the nurses to be very pleasant and respectful to the doctors. I think it was because I myself was once a nurse that I wanted the consideration and respect to be mutual between doctors and nurses. I greatly appreciated a pleasant doctor nurse relationship and I did not want this young and foolish, new attending physician to jeopardize the agreeable associations. In hindsight, I believe Dr. Inept felt insecure around me. Even though I was a second year resident, her position as my supervising attending physician seemed frail because I actually had more clinical experience than she had. It was also apparent that her diagnostic skills were not impressive. Her favorite residents were clearly those who 'kissed up to her' and that did not include me. Dr. Inept and I clashed from the start. For example, she would insist that we residents draw squares on a piece of paper to represent procedures and tests which had been ordered on patients and she insisted we check off the little boxes as test and lab results were obtained. I had my own effective method to follow tests and procedures which had been ordered on patients and I can assure you it did not consist of drawing and checking off little boxes! I preferred my approach over hers because most results were obtained in a timely manner and it was a scant few results that needed additional efforts to chase them down. Dr. Inept was warm and friendly to those residents who adopted her recommendations, and they even seemed to find that drawing the little boxes was helpful to them. However, she was outright abrasive towards me and it was evident that she did not appreciate my maverick personality. Likewise, I did not appreciate her attempts to teach as if it was Kindergarten school!

Dr. Dave Alexander was the chief pediatric attending physician and he supervised both the residents and Dr. Inept. I was pleased that, unlike Dr. Inept, he did not insist residents use little boxes drawn on paper to monitor for test results and he enjoyed a respectful working relationship with the nursing staff. When Dr. Inept was not present Dr. Alexander supervised us and I found the medical information Dr. Alexander shared with residents to be useful. I remember an incident when Dr. Alexander joined Dr. Inept and residents to supervise the medical care of a little boy that was admitted to the pediatric floor with a high fever and his chest x-ray revealed pneumonia. Dr. Inept insisted that antibiotics were not appropriate because the x-ray appearance 'looked like it was viral pneumonia'. I personally found her medical decision to be incongruent with good logic. After all, what if it was bacterial pneumonia and the little boy died simply because antibiotics were withheld? When Dr. Alexander was informed by Dr. Inept that she had not started antibiotics on this little boy with pneumonia because the appearance of the pneumonia on the x-ray 'looked like viral pneumonia', he was no longer the relaxed and calm doctor I had come to know. He was now livid, and he expressed utter disbelief at her ridiculous and irrational decision. He openly questioned her outside of the little boy's hearing range but in front of the residents, why she had withheld a potentially life saving treatment to this boy and put him at risk of dying unnecessarily while hospitalized. I was relieved to have Dr. Alexander around because Dr. Inept would ignore my recommendations as she was my direct supervisor, but she could not ignore Dr. Alexander's recommendations. I was always grateful to have Dr. Alexander on board because he frequently reversed inappropriate medical decisions which had been made by Dr. Inept. She seemed to be dependent on practicing medicine by following 'how to' directions written by an expert in a medical textbook for each medical diagnosis. Her method did not allow for individualization of each particular medical situation. Rather than using a medical textbook as a guide, she would treat it as gospel and she seemed incapable of using good common sense and sound judgment. I was most unfortunate that this individual was my direct supervisor and I was looking forward, more and more eagerly with each passing day, to the completion of this particular rotation.

Before this rotation was over I had the rare opportunity to diagnose a case of Munchausen-by-proxy Syndrome, but I was frustrated because my diagnosis was completely ignored by Dr. Inept. The situation involved a five month old baby boy that was admitted because of vague, but potentially serious symptoms, which the mother had reported to the baby's doctor. The baby was admitted to hospital to have the symptoms and signs evaluated. The mother was approximately forty years old and she was attractive and pleasant. On one evening during the hospitalization the mother reported to me that the baby had not urinated for many hours. The five month old baby boy appeared alert and well but I had to perform a suprapubic catheterization to evaluate his mother's report of the lack of urination further. This procedure consists of piercing the skin of the lower abdomen to enter the baby's bladder to obtain a urine sample. When I saw the pale yellow and very normal appearing urine flow into the catheter tubing, I became suspicious that the baby's mother was not being truthful about her baby's various medical signs and symptoms. I told the nurse that assisted me with the catheterization to observe the baby's hospital room for hidden wet diapers and I told her to call me immediately if she found any. I was working a thirty six hour shift in the hospital at the time and I remember I was called by the diligent nurse at about three a.m. The nurse informed me she had found several wet diapers hidden at the bottom of the trash container in the baby's room. Meanwhile, the nurse said the mother was still insisting the baby had produced no wet diapers. The next morning the baby was to be transferred to the Children's Hospital of

Philadelphia (CHOP), and further testing and evaluation was to be performed on this baby because of symptoms which were being reported by the mother. I prepared myself for an unpleasant conversation with the baby's mother and then I directly confronted her, albeit gently, and informed her that we had found the wet diapers. She didn't cry as I had expected her to. In fact, she appeared matter of fact and as cool as a cucumber when she confessed to the nurse and me that she was hiding the diapers and reporting fabricated medical problems because the baby's father had gone fishing against her wishes and he had left her alone. I reported the new developments to Dr. Inept and, incredulously, she ignored my report and she continued the transfer arrangements of the baby as if nothing had changed! The arrangements for further testing were to evaluate the baby for seizures which were a new condition reported by the mother. I was troubled that Dr. Inept was ignoring the new turn of events I had reported and she was instead choosing to continue the medical testing of the baby based on the symptoms and signs reported by the mother. I documented my findings carefully in the baby's hospital record and I informed the CHOP resident that was taking over the baby's medical care of my findings. I told the CHOP resident that this is now a case for social services and further medical testing of the baby is no longer appropriate. I advised the resident that this mother has admitted she has been lying about the baby's medical problems and that it is clear the baby's mother is in need of psychiatric evaluation and treatment and that she is a danger to her baby. I explained further that the mother had subjected the baby to potentially dangerous and invasive medical testing and treatments in an attempt to obtain attention from her husband.

Sadly, Dr. Inept had proved to me once again she had no business working in the field of medicine. In this situation she had willfully disregarded the wellbeing of a baby. It was apparent Dr. Inept preferred to pursue the easier route of medical testing of a well baby because she simply did not want to pursue the difficult social issues of the situation.

To top off my pediatric rotation cake with icing, I was presented with a substandard evaluation of my work. This evaluation had been completed by none other than Dr. Inept. I was surprised that she somehow related the fact that she was pregnant and that I was hoping to become pregnant to be a source of stress and difficulty in my relationship with her. On the contrary, I was happy that she was pregnant and this in no way made the situation psychologically difficult for me. I was not at all sure why she made this erroneous conclusion. Perhaps she would have had emotional difficulty if the situation had been reversed. She should not have mistakenly concluded that my reaction would mimic hers since it was apparent I was in no way like her, after all, I only choose to emulate those individuals I respect. I knew her unjust evaluation of me would not be of importance in the big scheme of my profession because my clinical rotation evaluations up to this point had all been outstanding. It was the principle of the matter that disturbed me. This incompetent self serving nincompoop had the gall to evaluate me in such a condescending manner and I was not about to sign off on this unjust evaluation without airing my grievance. I told my mentor, Dr. Val Pendley, of Dr. Inept's inappropriate behavior. Dr. Pendley listened to my complaints about my unpleasant experiences under Dr. Inept's thumb. She knew me well by now and she was aware of my past and the inappropriate verbal battering I had received from the arrogant Dr. Hotair. I appreciated her interest in my complaints and she added details of my account of blatant unfairness adjacent to Dr. Inept's unfair assessment of me. By this point in time, I enjoyed an excellent reputation within the residency program and Dr. Pendley accepted my assessment as an accurate representation. I was relieved to finally be independent of the incompetence of Dr. Inept.

Chapter 23 – I'm Pregnant!

About a third of the way through my final year of residency, Phil and I vacationed in Cape Cod, Massachusetts. We took the ferry to Martha's Vineyard and Nantucket and we had a wonderful time sight-seeing on these small, famous islands. About a week before we left for our vacation, Dr. Schinfeld informed Phil and me that it was time to begin more aggressive strategies to achieve pregnancy, since attempts so far had not been successful. Phil and I advised Dr. Schinfeld that we would put things on hold and I would stop taking the medicines to increase my fertility until we returned from our vacation. Phil was quite disturbed at the thought of more aggressive fertility procedures because I would be given additional hormonal medicines and he expressed concern that these may not be good for my health. Needless to say, on vacation, Phil seemed to be 'a man with a mission'. I, on the other hand, was my usual self. I mention this because, when it comes to an issue pertaining to infertility, the focus is almost always on the female. For example, I remember a preponderance of comments from concerned well-meaning individuals, such as, "You cannot get pregnant because of all the stress you are under." In reality, I did not feel at all stressed. On the contrary, I was actually learning from and enjoying the infertility evaluation and treatment process because I knew it would help me to be a more compassionate doctor in the future for my patients who were having infertility issues. On the way back from Nantucket, we had purchased first class tickets for the ferry. I was grateful for this because the weather had become cold and stormy and we were able to enjoy the comfort of a couch in the cozy enclosed space of the ferry. I was unusually exhausted and I slept during the return trip, stretched out on the couch. Phil was not as tired as I was even though we both had similar amounts of sleep and activities. In hindsight, I wondered if it was because my body was preparing for a biological change that it had never before experienced, something in fact that was very special, and that would change my life forever in a wonderful and meaningful way. Yes, you guessed it, I was pregnant! About one week before my period was due, I routinely checked a home pregnancy test, and it was usually negative. On this one occasion however, after returning home, the result was 'half positive'. I told Phil about the result and we knew that this test result was actually very significant since I had never seen anything but an outright negative pregnancy test prior to this. A few days later I notified Dr. Schinfeld of my positive pregnancy test. He appeared very concerned and he advised me not to spread this news to any other person except Phil. Dr. Schinfeld cautioned me that an early positive pregnancy test result unfortunately often changes to a negative result. He said this is because many pregnancies are lost in the very early stages, many times before a female even realizes she is pregnant. I confessed to Dr. Schinfeld that I was so excited about my first ever positive pregnancy test that I had already told my friends and family about the positive result. I explained to him that, even if the test does become negative, I was still very excited and happy to have become pregnant. At hearing this, Dr. Schinfeld looked at me disapprovingly. Fortunately, my fifty percent positive pregnancy test did indeed progress all the way to be a one hundred percent positive result.

Early in my pregnancy, an amniocentesis had been performed to evaluate our baby's condition. I was concerned during the procedure when I noticed Phil's face become very pale. Phil then began to perspire profusely as he witnessed a long needle pierce the skin of my abdominal wall. The needle was then directed in through the wall of my womb in order to obtain some amniotic fluid that surrounded our baby. I could see that Phil was going to faint and so I told him to put his head between his legs to improve the blood flow to his brain. Fortunately, Phil did not lose consciousness during the amniocentesis procedure. Several days later I was very excited when Dr. Schinfeld handed me a copy of our baby's sex chromosomes. They were XY chromosomes, which meant, of course, we were having a boy.

Phil and I brought a book filled with boys' names and we enjoyed the process of researching names for a boy. For example, both Phil and I liked the name 'Max' but then we decided against this name because I was concerned he would live up to a nick-name of 'Mad-Max' once he became a teenager! We finally settled on the name of Matthew because all of the Matthews we knew were nice individuals. We also like the meaning of the name 'Matthew', because it means 'Gift from God'. Dr. Mike Brown, a resident in my residency program, arranged a surprise baby shower for me. He was very creative with the arrangements and I was thrilled that he even included the name 'Matthew' on the cake for my shower.

Chapter 24 – Moonlighting

I had begun moonlighting early in the second year of my residency at a medical office located outside of Abington, Pa. This was located about a half hour's drive from my home in Oreland. Moonlighting during residency was a common practice for residents because it helped residents to locate a suitable position for employment at the end of their residency period. I had very little contact with the doctors in the group but I enjoyed the moonlighting position because the nursing staff and the patients were appreciative of my help and also because the work was fast-paced. The work, however, did become more challenging once I developed 'morning sickness' each evening, instead of in the mornings! I believe I frequently felt sicker than the patients I was treating for their various ailments and I was often relieved at the end of each moonlighting session that I had managed to complete the evening of work without vomiting! At the tail end of my first trimester I was thankful that my morning sickness had finally resolved.

I touched bases with the contact person in the group, Dr. Peter Schmuck, about a future full time position in the group at the completion of my residency. Dr. Schmuck, Phil and I had a meeting at Tiffany's Restaurant in Center Square to discuss the expectations and requirements of an associate position in the group. Dr. Schmuck had a similar appearance to Charley Chaplin because he had a thick black moustache and he was short. He surprised me because it was obvious he considered himself to be highly attractive. At this meeting, Dr. Schmuck was business like and pleasant. Unfortunately, Phil and I later came to realize that the reasonable work schedule Dr. Schmuck described and said I would have was actually the schedule that only the physician owners enjoyed. I'm sure Dr. Schmuck realized that I would never have accepted a position in the group if he had been up front and honest with me about the real expectations of the schedule. I came to realize that new physicians were expected to work a 'boot camp' like schedule and I was as angry as a swatted hornet when I realized he had been deceitful in our initial discussions about my schedule.

Since I was under the false impression that the schedule would be reasonable and therefore conducive to the additional challenges of motherhood, I had a meeting with the three owners of the practice. We met at a local restaurant in Chestnut Hill to discuss my future employment with the group. I was disturbed by Dr. Schmuck's abhorrent behavior at the meeting because he made lewd comments about our young, attractive waitress. I was especially repulsed because I knew he was supposedly happily married with two small children. It was evident to me that Dr. Schmuck was an advocate of the chauvinistic male double standard. Even though I was aware of Dr. Schmuck's level of immaturity, I accepted a position as a new associate within the group because I needed a job, and also because the remaining two doctors in the group seemed reasonable, especially the most senior group member. I am a realist and I recognized that no matter where I located employment, it was unlikely that I would find a position in which I would be completely satisfied with all of the associates in the group.

I was now in my third trimester of pregnancy and Phil and I were both surprised that I had developed a voracious appetite like I had never experienced before. My stomach had become a bottomless pit for food once my morning sickness had resolved. Instead of eating for two I ate like I was eating for four! Phil and I frequented The International House of Pancakes, and our favorite meal was a large helping of breakfast, no matter what time of the day it was. We would take half of each other's food so we had more variety on our plates. Prior to my pregnancy, Phil's healthy appetite was ordinarily kept in check by my normally controlled appetite, but now it seemed things were out of control as my appetite seemed to mimic his. Before my pregnancy, I had never had to concern myself with weight gain because I was slim and I never gained a pound. Needless to say, despite my small, five foot two inch, one hundred and twenty five pound, pre-pregnancy frame, I had gained a whopping sixty pounds by the end of my pregnancy. I attributed this to the change in my brain hunger setting and, not surprisingly, I developed gestational diabetes. I chose to treat the diabetes aggressively under the supervision of an Endocrinologist because I knew this would be important for the optimum health of our baby. I immediately reduced my caloric intake despite my hunger pangs and I monitored my blood sugar closely.

Because my blood sugars remained higher that optimum, my Endocrinologist prescribed insulin for me and he kept a close watch on my blood sugar readings. My pregnancy was, just by chance, perfectly timed such that I would have our baby at the end of my residency. In the case of a pregnancy complicated by gestational diabetes, it is usual procedure to intervene and induce delivery of the baby if spontaneous delivery has not occurred by the normal due date. The reason for this is to protect the baby from any reduction in blood flow through the umbilical cord which can occur at the tail end of a pregnancy when a condition such as diabetes is present. My obstetrician, Dr. Crispino, decided to induce my pregnancy for delivery close to my due date. He explained he wanted to guard against this potential reduction in blood flow through the umbilical cord as my due date neared. It just so happened that my admission to Chestnut Hill Hospital to induce delivery of the baby was scheduled on the same day that the dinner to congratulate graduating family medicine residents was to be held. Keep in mind that I was one of the two graduating residents which were to be honored at this dinner. Dr. Mebane, the program director, appeared quite unhappy when he was informed that I may not be able to attend the dinner because of my scheduled delivery date. He knew, however, that it would not be wise to delay my delivery, and it was also too late to change the date of the residents' dinner.

Chapter 25 – Delivery

At six o' clock in the morning on June 5th 1992, Phil, my mother and I were instructed to arrive at the hospital. I took along a cake bearing the words, 'Happy Birthday Matthew and Dr. Crispino!' I had been told by a staff nurse a few days earlier that it was Dr. Crispino's birthday on June 5th and so I had this birthday cake made to celebrate this special day of two important people. Even though I was not allowed to have any food or drink in case I would require emergency surgery, I knew I would enjoy watching the cake get devoured by Dr. Crispino, the hospital staff and my family.

I arrived at the hospital promptly at 6am and was told to slip into the cotton hospital gown. I was both a little scared and excited. A nurse set up my intravenous infusion and I was given some medicine called Pitocin to induce uterine contractions. As the contractions increased in intensity, the Anesthesiologist gave me an epidural injection so that I would not suffer with the intense contractions induced by the Pitocin. Unfortunately, the epidural injection gave me pain relief on only one side of my body and I experienced intense contractions on the opposite side. I knew this should not be so and so I called for the Anesthesiologist to reposition the epidural catheter. This was successful and I was grateful to have relief from the pain so that I could return to my main business of enjoying this long awaited, very special day.

The residency dinner was held in my absence on June 5th 1992 but I knew I was in the attendees' thoughts. This is because we had frequent phone calls from Dr. Mike Brown who was in attendance at the dinner, and he was keeping everybody at the dinner informed about the progress of my delivery, or, as it turned out, the lack of progress. As the evening progressed, things were not looking good because my cervix had not dilated beyond three centimeters out of the necessary ten centimeters for several hours, even though Dr. Crispino had broken my water to try to get things moving. It was becoming late and I saw some indication that Matthew was becoming distressed. I saw some irregularity of Matthew's heart beat as I glanced over at the paper print-out of his heart rhythm. The nurse saw me evaluating the paper print-outs and she quickly snatched them from my hand so that I could no longer see them. It was clear she was aware Matthew was becoming distressed and she did not want me to be concerned about my baby's developing fatigue since she knew I would worry about this. She explained that I needed to be a patient at this time and not a doctor. She was right.

It was now about eight o'clock in the evening and Dr. Crispino came to my room to speak to me. He recommended a cesarean section since I had not progressed beyond three centimeters and Matthew was showing signs of fatigue. I accepted his recommendation without hesitation as I knew it was in my baby's best interest. Phil and I had chosen Dr. Mebane to be Matthew's doctor much earlier in my pregnancy. When a cesarean section is to be performed, the baby's doctor must be called in to attend the delivery in case there is an emergency. It was therefore necessary for Dr. Mebane, the head of the residency program and the main speaker at the dinner, to leave the residents' dinner while it was in full swing in order to attend my cesarean section. What a troublemaker I had become! Even so, Dr. Mebane did not seem at all unhappy about the circumstances. He was smiling and he seemed honored to be present at the time that our baby boy was to be born. I lay on the table feeling dependent and vulnerable, looking up at my caregivers as the doctors prepared to open my womb to deliver my precious little package.

I was fortunate to be awake and alert during my cesarean section. Phil later told me he wanted to look over the drape to watch the surgeons operate on me. He said he was very curious and he wanted to watch the surgeons take Matthew out from my womb. He remembered his prior experience during my amniocentesis procedure when he almost fainted, but this did not deter him from watching this miraculous event unfold before his eyes. He was eager to be available to hold his precious newborn son immediately after he was born. Phil, my mom and I were all smiling broadly when we heard the healthy cries of our newborn boy, Matthew Kyle Hoffman. Dr. Mebane took Matthew from Dr. Crispino, and he carefully examined Matthew to make sure all his parts were present and intact. He then dried Matthew gently with warm, cotton blankets and he handed our precious son to his ecstatic and proud Father. I unfortunately felt pain as I was being stitched back together and the medicine I was given to relieve the pain caused me to vomit. This in turn, caused more pain! Naturally, this was quite unpleasant but it was soon over. This ordeal had all been worthwhile as I cradled the precious little package that I now had in my arms. I was taken to my room shortly after this to rest and Matthew was initially taken to the nursery to be observed by the nurses.

That first night in the hospital, a nurse brought Matthew to my room because he was crying. She suggested I try breastfeeding him and so I placed Matthew's mouth gently to my nipple. Matthew had difficulty latching onto my breasts because of their large size. I was very upset when the nurse forcibly pushed Matthew's face into my breast thinking that somehow this would encourage him to breast feed. Instead, my poor helpless son was gasping for air in between his cries, and he flailed his arms and legs because he was being asphyxiated by my breast. It was at this crucial moment in time that I met my new instinct, my powerful and protective maternal instinct. I was livid at this particular nurse because of her frank stupidity. This foolish nurse was ordering me to suffocate my son on my breast and it was past time that I ordered her OUT of my room, immediately! I also told her never to step foot in my room again.

After I had ordered this incompetent nurse out of the room and the atmosphere was tranquil, the wonderful bonding process between mother and baby began. We enjoyed the serenity and the quietness of the night. I held him gently and I brought him up close to my breast. We relaxed together as if we had all the time in the world and we were peaceful. My son soon learned the skill of breastfeeding as nature intended, without duress, and in his own relaxed time. Over the next few days I began to produce a bountiful supply of nutritious breast milk. I was fortunate in that I was able to breast feed Matthew until he was fifteen months old even though I had to start work full time when he was just six weeks old. When Matthew was fifteen months old he became disinterested in breast feeding and I stopped lactating without difficulty because, by this age, he was only breast feeding one time daily at his bedtime.

Chapter 26 – Work Disaster!

I wanted to stay home with Matthew longer than six weeks but I began my work as a family doctor because I had to begin payment of my medical school student loans. Nothing could have prepared me for the gut wrenching emotion I experienced the first day that I dropped Matthew off at the daycare. I felt dire guilt that I had to leave him there. I was fortunate because the daycare was wonderful and the baby room had a particularly compassionate and loving worker named Thelma who cared for her four babies as if they were her own flesh and blood.

Unfortunately, Dr. Schmuck made my return to work a very unpleasant experience. It was his responsibility to make up the doctors' work schedule and he showed no compassion whatsoever for a doctor and a new mother who is returning to work. It was apparent to me that he possessed zero empathy and his behavior was reprehensible. I was furious as I looked over my work schedule because he had scheduled me with twice the number of hours he had told me I would be working when he explained my work schedule to me at our initial dinner meeting. As I mentioned earlier, Dr. Schmuck only now explained to me that the new doctors are given the 'boot camp schedule', with no regard to my responsibility as a new mother! I was concerned about my availability to Matthew and I was not about to let any person compromise my relationship with him. I had brought Matthew into this world and I had every intention of fulfilling all of my responsibilities to him.

Another doctor, Dr. Kathy Graham, had completed her residency and she had applied to Dr. Schmuck's group at the same time that I had applied. The senior doctors had hired both of us, probably because of the low starting salary and also because we were both good workers. It was written in our contracts that there would be an increase in our salary of $10,000.00 each year, over a six year period. Again, this wasn't very competitive in the marketplace, but I was personally drawn to this medical practice because of the meaningful relationships I had developed with many of the patients. I complained to Kathy that the schedule is different than promised and it is not acceptable to me because I need to be available for my son. I expressed my frustration and anger that I had been lied to by Dr. Schmuck. She responded that if I leave the practice then she will also leave. It now occurred to me that part of Kathy's appeal to join this practice was that I would also be joining the group. I was furious at being messed around in this fashion and so I called Dr. Schmuck and chewed him out on the phone because he had not been honest with me about the schedule. I announced I would not continue to work at his office because I am scheduled for double the number of work hours than I was promised! I advised him that Kathy says she will also leave if I leave. The three owners met with me and Kathy emergently to try to appease us. It was clear the senior doctors did not want me to quit, after all I was a dedicated and diligent worker that already had earned a positive reputation among the patients. The senior doctors announced that I could have the schedule I had been originally promised but I was told that I would have to agree to some financial concessions. These concessions were unquestionably unfair, given I was simply expecting to have the schedule I had been promised in the first place. By the end of the meeting, I had consented to continue to work at their office because it was the simplest of my options at the time, given I had my monthly medical school loans to pay. Kathy also agreed to stay, but she agreed to accept the heavier schedule and she therefore had no concessions. Kathy was able to manage the heavier schedule because her home situation was quite different from mine. Her husband was a disabled police officer and he was therefore able to be a stay at home dad for their children. Phil and I, on the other hand, both had to work, if for no other reason than to pay off our college tuition loans. Neither Phil nor I had been fortunate enough to have parents who were able to help defray our tuition costs, and so the financial costs were now bearing down on us like the weight of an anchor. Still, my powerful maternal instinct was in full force and I was determined I would be available for Matt. At the same time, I enjoyed my profession as a family doctor. The field of medicine is a 'feel good field'; at the end of each day I can reflect on how many patients I have been fortunate to have impacted in a positive way. I knew I was very fortunate to have my precious son and also to have the opportunity to be a doctor for so many wonderful patients.

My schedule now almost matched the senior doctors' schedule, although admittedly, my schedule was more burdensome than theirs. This is because many non-urgent visits were added on to my schedule beyond ten pm. It is a fact that at this late time, I would gladly evaluate an anxious patient who requires an emergency evaluation of, for example, chest pain. I, however, would often be very frustrated because I would be required to evaluate a patient at this time of night that had, for example, foot pain of more than three month's duration. I never considered this to be the patient's inappropriateness, after all, who can blame the patient for accepting an appointment that is offered to him or her, even if it is very late at night? I knew Dr. Schmuck was behind my frustrating schedule and Phil told me I should talk to Dr. Schmuck about this as he is sure he will understand the problem and fix it. Phil was surprised when I told him that Dr. Schmuck thinks the schedule is fine just the way it is, even when I told Dr. Schmuck that I would look for a position elsewhere if he does not make the schedule reasonable. I found this was the nature of this practice, boot camp for the new bright eyed and bushy tailed doctors, while the senior doctors enjoyed their more leisurely, highly desirable schedule. This was grossly unfair for the new and unsuspecting doctors that joined the group.

Another situation I was most uncomfortable with had to do with the care my patients were allowed to have. Specifically, if a patient requested a referral to see a chiropractor, the request was denied, citing this was not a medically necessary treatment. Although I personally had no need to visit a chiropractor, two of the senior doctors within the practice visited a chiropractor regularly. I knew this was extremely hypocritical and unfair, but I was told referrals to chiropractors were not to be given because this was the practice's rule. I was uncomfortable that I was not allowed to permit my patients to receive chiropractic care when they requested it and many patients expressed their dissatisfaction with this decision.

It had been apparent to Phil that I had been dissatisfied in my work at this practice for a long time, but he had been unaware of the full

106

extent of the difficulties I was experiencing. A turning point and an eye opener for Phil came when he witnessed Dr. Schmuck deny my request for a change in my unjust schedule. Phil was surprised at the smug attitude I received from Dr. Schmuck and his total inflexibility with my request. On the other hand, I was not at all surprised; I fully expected the selfish response that I received. Up until this point in time, Phil had not taken my complaints seriously. It was after Phil heard my conversation with Dr. Schmuck on the phone that it was crystal clear to him why I was dissatisfied. The blatant lack of fairness this group demonstrated toward their new physicians was intolerable and Phil and I agreed there was no future for me with this group of self interested doctors. It was well past time for me to look for work elsewhere.

Chapter 27 – Moving On

I noticed an advertisement in a local medical paper for a doctor to join a family medicine group located in King of Prussia. Although there were other advertisements describing opportunities in the area, this one advertisement was of particular interest to me because I liked the location. I called the medical office to express my interest and I was told to expect a call from one of the doctors in the group that evening and at seven pm, the phone rang. The doctor had a pleasant and deep voice. I told him I was moving to the King of Prussia area and I was in need of employment. I had decided it was not appropriate to go into further detail on the phone at this time, especially since this was so early in the process. He described some details of the practice and the type of doctoring they do and it sounded surprisingly similar to my current workplace. I felt I would be ideally suited to the position and I eagerly accepted his invitation to interview with the group. We decided on a meeting later that week at nine pm. This may seem like a strange time to meet but it was convenient given the late evening hours of many doctors.

I met with the doctors in King of Prussia after their evening hours at about nine pm, as we had arranged. Dr. Tommy Lamp greeted me as I entered the attractive medical office and he escorted me into the conference room. He was friendly, short and slim with a beard, and he led the meeting. Dr. Bill Ward was taller with a mustache and he too had a pleasant, friendly and relaxed disposition. Dr. Maria Kith was one of the female doctors and she, like the other female doctor in this group, was pleasant with a professional temperament. Dr. Sherianne May was tall and slender and she did not have hours that evening. She arrived a little late for the meeting, very apologetic.

It was a remarkable meeting. I was honest with the group members about my dissatisfaction with my current associates. Bill seemed a little upset that I had not told him of my discontent with my current situation when I had spoken with him on the phone prior to the meeting. I told him I did not feel it was appropriate to speak of my disgruntlement until we all met face to face. I explained that fairness is a quality I hold in high regard and I described how unfair the work schedule was compared to that which I had been promised. I told them of the fixed reasonable schedule we agreed upon in exchange for a reduced income and that this was acceptable to me so I would not compromise my prime responsibility which was to care for my son. I confessed that my work will always be second in importance to my duty to my son, but that I will work very diligently and professionally with them.

I had completed my explanation as to why I was looking for a new professional position. It was now time for these doctors to explain to me why they were looking for a new associate. They explained that the practice was initially opened by Dr. Harkulus. Dr. Lamp and Dr. Harkulus had attended the same medical residency program together. Dr. Lamp joined Dr. Harkulus at the practice after he had completed his residency, which was one year after Dr. Harkulus had opened the medical office. Dr. Ward told me he was tired of being a solo practitioner and so he closed his office in order to join Dr. Harkulus and Dr. Lamp. After she had completed her residency program Dr. Kith joined the group. These four doctors were owners of the practice. Dr. May advised me she had joined the group more recently and she therefore was not yet a full partner. Dr. May and Dr. Kith had attended the same residency program and they both completed their residency at the same time. Dr. May had joined a medical group initially elsewhere but she was not happy and so she left that group to join the doctors here in King of Prussia. Dr. May later confided in me that she too had experienced an initial unpleasant employment situation similar to mine, and so she certainly understood and agreed with my decision to change employment.

Dr. Kith told me the four doctors essentially became uncomfortable with Dr. Harkulus's work in their group for business reasons. Dr. Kith explained further she could no longer tolerate the situation and so she gave her colleagues an ultimatum. Either Dr. Harkulus had to go or she would leave the group. The colleagues chose to oust Dr. Harkulus from the practice with the help of their attorney. This left open a position to fill within the group and hence the newspaper advertisement to which I responded. But wait; there's more. Dr. Harkulus owned a little over fifty percent of the professional building in which the practice was located and he opened his own medical office directly across from his ex-partners' office! It is true that most applicants for this position would have turned and run at this point, but I was sufficiently unhappy with my current situation that I remained interested. In addition, the twist of drama that had been presented to me attracted me even more to this group. I was also impressed that these doctors were honest in describing their current situation so openly to me. By the end of the evening, we were interested in going forward, and I was told to expect an offer of employment as soon as a contract could be drawn up.

As promised, I promptly received an offer to join the group of doctors in King of Prussia. The contract included a fair and generous offer which I gladly accepted and signed with great pleasure. Needless to say, my old associates were not at all happy that I was leaving. They complained I should have given more than two weeks notice to the group I was leaving as I had not allowed them time to make arrangements to cover my schedule. I retorted I had given ample notice to Dr. Schmuck over six months ago when I advised him I would leave if the many instances of unfairness and lack of respect I was constantly subjected to continued. There was a look of surprise on the faces of the doctors upon hearing this and so I explained further that it had been the straw that broke the camel's back when Dr. Schmuck refused to stop adding non-emergency patients to my schedule after ten pm. I explained further that I had no objection to extending my schedule for an emergently ill patient, but to constantly have my schedule extended late at night for patients with minor chronic ailments was abuse of my employment by the group. Then to have my appeals for a more reasonable schedule disregarded and instead to be smugly advised that, "The schedule is fine the way it is" was flat out infuriating! Was it possible that Dr. Schmuck had not passed this information on to his two partners? At this point it made no difference because I was moving on.

The day after I had announced to the group I was leaving, Phil was astounded because he received a phone call from Dr. Schmuck, supposedly to express concern about my wellbeing. This phone call was truly condescending. Since Dr. Schmuck had not cared about my wellbeing in my years working in his group prior to this, why would he suddenly care now? He told Phil I did not know what I was getting myself into by joining this group of doctors in King of Prussia. Dr. Schmuck explained to Phil he and Dr. Harkulus had been friends dating back to their residency, and so he claimed to know many troubling details of the new group I was joining. When Phil told Dr. Schmuck the group had already provided me with all of these 'troubling details', he was clearly surprised. Phil considered the phone call he received from Dr. Schmuck highly offensive and chauvinistic because he said Dr. Schmuck should have had the decency to speak directly to me and not to him. I told Phil not to be in the least bit surprised since this was behavior typical of Dr. Schmuck. The senior associates asked me if there was something that could be done to change my mind about leaving the group. It was clear my requests for fairness would now be considered whereas previously my requests simply fell on deaf ears. I acknowledged to myself it was past time for me to leave this group. I knew I did not share the general philosophy of the doctors in this group. Clearly, I would never abuse a new doctor in the same manner that the doctors are accustomed to treating their new young doctors. Fundamentally, I did not agree with a boot camp approach for a new associate and I would never be comfortable being part of this unfair mentality. I anticipated my new colleagues in King of Prussia would suit me much better!

I notified my patients that I was leaving for reasons to do with location because my employers requested that I do not discuss the unfairness I had experienced while working with them. Many patients, however, told me during their patient visits with me, that they knew I was leaving because I was not treated well by the senior doctors in the group. They acknowledged that they knew this because there were many doctors who had left before me for this reason. I would just smile and change the subject. The senior doctors were visibly relieved that I did not openly discuss my employment dissatisfaction with patients. I was concerned for some of my patients who had requested to switch from the most senior doctor to my care. It was the official policy of this doctor to refuse to allow his patients to change to the care of another doctor within the group. Some of his patients complained to me they felt intimidated and berated by him during their office visits and they had switched over to my care, despite his policy to deny patients the right to change to a different doctor in the group. The patients told me they appreciated my kinder and gentler approach when I addressed issues such as a patient's excess weight or a patient's lack of exercise. I was now concerned because I felt as if I was abandoning these patients by leaving the practice. However, I could no longer tolerate the abuse from the senior doctors and still maintain my dignity and my self respect. It was clear I had to leave this demeaning work environment. I recommended to my patients that after I leave they become patients of the other female physician in the group. She was well respected and also a compassionate physician. I was confident my patients would be comfortable and satisfied under her medical care.

Chapter 28 – Our Son Matt

By this time, as I started my new job in King of Prussia, Matt was four years old. On one particular day that I remember well, I arrived at the daycare to take him home at the end of the day. I was immediately disturbed to find Matthew, appearing dejected, sitting on a wooden step in the playground. He was sobbing quietly to himself and a mixture of tears and dirt trickled down his cheeks. I wrapped my arms around Matt to comfort him and I asked him why he was upset. He told me, between sobs, that Ms. Cruella had taken away his cup filled with acorns. I walked over to Hannah, the teacher's aide, and I asked why my son was crying. She seemed relieved by my question and she told me she was extremely frustrated by the incompetence of Cruella, and that taking a cup filled with acorns from a kid was the last straw. She explained that Cruella, Matt's baccalaureate degree teacher, had taken the cup from him that he had proudly filled with acorns he had collected from the playground. Hannah told me that Cruella had also reprimanded Matt for using the cup, 'to litter in the playground'. She went on to say that Cruella's behavior was ridiculous and she said she could no longer tolerate Cruella's bullying of the children. She claimed she would be speaking to Donna, the director of the daycare, about Cruella's mean- spirited management of the children. I was livid to hear how inappropriately Cruella had treated my child and I told Hannah not to worry, she didn't have to speak to Donna about this incident because I would be speaking to her. My fiercely protective maternal instinct was proving to be alive and well and I was enraged by what I had been told. I proceeded into the school to locate Donna and I found her collecting items from the storage closet. She appeared concerned because I was clearly angry at the information Hannah had given me, and she was unable to get past me to exit the closet. I described the inappropriate management of Matt by Cruella and I complained she obviously has chosen the wrong line of work for herself because she doesn't have a understand appropriate management of children. I explained further, and she knew I was correct, that a child should be encouraged to appreciate nature by collecting acorns. I continued that the concern Cruella had that Matt was littering in the playground was ridiculous, and it underscores her deficiency in knowledge of child development. I insisted that Cruella should be fired because she is not competent to provide child care. It was clear my argument was strong and I also had an additional staff member to serve as a witness to back me up. I knew that Donna cared deeply about the well being of all the children enrolled at her school and she concluded that Cruella could not be trusted to provide care in this loving and nurturing school. The next day I was advised by Donna that Cruella had handed in her resignation. I expect there had been several cases of mismanagement of the children by Cruella because I know it is rare that an employee is fired based on a single incident. I think Hannah was relieved that I addressed the situation with Donna because, as a teacher's aide, Hannah may not have had the influence that I had as a parent. Children are innocent and they are dependent on adults to love and nurture them and also to have those adults step up to the plate to protect them when situations such as this arise. Similarly, schools staff members should always behave in a professional manner and encourage parents and caregivers to communicate any concerns they have about the care their child is receiving with the school. Each situation can be addressed thoughtfully and carefully so as to maintain optimum care for each child. My personal example in this case demonstrates the school protected the wellbeing of my child as soon as I provided details of the mean spirited Cruella to Donna.

On a lighter note, on another day at the daycare as I arrived at the school to take Matt home, he told me he had watched a football game on TV and he had not enjoyed it. He was very indignant that the 'grown-ups' fight over a ball and he told me, "They do not share the ball!" I smiled and I pondered the fact that this is how a football game must appear to a four or five year old child; grown-ups that behave badly and do not do what we always tell our children they should do, they should always share the ball!

It was about this time, also at the daycare, that Matt became a vegetarian. The teacher told me she had given a lesson about food and that she had explained to the children where we get meat from. Matt's teacher told me he was very upset to learn that meat comes from animals and that we have to kill animals in order to eat meat. From hereon, Matt has refused to eat meat, even to this day! I know this is an unusual situation because Phil and I both eat meat; in fact one of our favorite dishes is a lean and juicy steak. I am patiently waiting for Matt to wake up one day and realize he is missing out on many mouth watering, tasty delights. I closely monitored his diet to ensure it included all the necessary nutritional components along with adequate protein. Matt is six foot two inches tall and he reached this height before turning fifteen so it is clear he received adequate nutrients despite his objection to meat!

Many called Matt the 'gentle giant'. I know I am very fortunate to have such a wonderful, affectionate and caring son. In school he was conscientious and diligent. A parent could not want for a nicer son and Phil and I are very grateful to have him. Once, when my Mother was visiting from Pittsburgh, she asked Matt if he would like to have a special girlfriend in his life. Matt smiled and he put his arm around my shoulder and said, "My mother is my special girlfriend." This was a side of Matt that my mother had not seen before. It was a very sweet moment, one which demonstrated our special mother and son relationship. Naturally, Phil and I are looking forward to becoming grandparents in the future. Since this time, a special friend has entered Matt's life and it is our pleasure to welcome her with open arms!

Chapter 29 – New Employment

Meanwhile, I experienced a pleasant change at my new job in King of Prussia. All of the doctors worked the same scheduled hours and there was no such thing as 'boot camp' for the new doctor. I was fairly busy immediately and when I had some time in my schedule I would work on methods designed to improve the practice. For example, I had a concern that patient phone calls to address their medical issues taken by staff members needed to be addressed more carefully. Here is a case in point: I would be handed a note from a staff person that a patient with a headache had called and the patient is asking for medical advice. I would be provided with the patient's medical chart and I would be expected to make a medical recommendation based on this limited information. The fact that the patient had a headache was the only information I would be given about the patient's symptoms. I was aware that this information was inadequate for a doctor to make an informed medical decision for the patient that would ensure the patient would come to no harm. To overcome this problem for the patient and for the practice staff I created a template that served as a guide for the staff to use. This template listed the many common different ailments that were treated by the doctors such as headache, abdominal pain, urinary infection and respiratory illness. I included on this guide the questions a physician would typically ask a patient about their ailment if they were physically present in the office. The result was a significant improvement in the mechanism by which phone calls from patients who had medical questions were handled. Under this new and improved system, when a patient with a medical problem called the office, the nurse or medical assistant would ask the patient questions from my printed guide sheet which pertained to their particular illness, such as, 'is a fever present?' or, 'is the headache the worst headache of your life?' The staff member would then pass on the completed sheet to the patient's doctor who could now make a more informed decision about the best course of action to take. For example, the doctor may recommend the patient to take some Tylenol and schedule an office visit the next day, or, the instructions may be to recommend the patient must call for an ambulance immediately. I remember Dr. Kith was not in favor of my phone call guide sheet. She complained that it was impractical to use because it tied up staff members to an excessive degree on the phone. However, the nurses and medical assistants told me they greatly appreciated the sheet because it provided them with guidance to help them assess a patient's illness more cautiously. I suspect that I thought up the idea to develop the guide sheet because of my unique experience as both a nurse and a physician. Through my prior experience as a nurse, I was better able to understand the concerns of the nurses and medical assistants who wanted improved communication between the patients and the doctors because the nurses and medical assistants knew this would benefit patients. The phone call symptom guide sheet quickly became an integral part of the daily office function despite Dr. Kith's objection to it. The nurses and medical assistants unanimously expressed they were more confident because of the guidance they were able to acquire from my phone call symptom sheet when patients called with their symptoms of illness. I was pleased that the phone call symptom guide sheet was appreciated by the staff members and I knew it was highly protective for, not only my patients, but also for all of the patients in the medical practice because it was formally embraced as a standard of care.

I went on to create another aide for the office. However, I was the only doctor to adopt this aide, probably because I tailored it to my medical treatment style. I have always disliked redundancy in general and there is a lot of redundancy in medicine, such as writing the same prescription many times over. Let me explain the redundancy by citing a particular example of it. A patient who calls with symptoms of a urinary tract infection would have one of my phone call symptom guide sheets completed by the medical assistant, and then the symptom sheet would be handed to me to determine the appropriate medical management. Many times this medical management would be identical for a given diagnosis. Herein lay redundancy and I concluded I could potentially eliminate unnecessary work. I therefore created my second sheet, which I coined a treatment sheet. This treatment sheet listed multiple diagnoses, such as, Upper Respiratory Infection or Acute

Gastroenteritis. Beneath each ailment was a numbered-alphabetical system which included my usual prescription/treatments for each ailment along with the general symptomatic care recommendations. This proved to be of great benefit, not only for me, but also for the nurses and medical assistants. They could read the print without difficulty because it was not hand written. For a patient who called with symptoms of simple gastroenteritis and the patient had recently visited the office and therefore preferred no office visit, for example, I would simply write, '16A'. The medical assistant would implement all of my treatment recommendations listed for 16A. I had created a full treatment sheet with my common treatment recommendations for the majority of ailments that patients would frequently call about. Once again, the nurses and medical assistants unanimously were in favor of adopting this legible treatment sheet because it provided benefits for my patients and also for the nurses and medical assistants. Also my recommendations were complete in that they included all symptomatic measures that were added for each problem to help my patients to get better and faster medical care. This was once again a win-win-win situation for the patient, the nurses and medical assistants, and for me, the doctor.

Chapter 30 – Sell out!

I was overall content and satisfied working in the medical practice at King of Prussia because my new colleagues were reasonable to work with. It was about this time that the large health systems were purchasing small and independent medical group practices. Dr. Kith frequently repeated her position that she would never agree to sell our practice to a large health organization. You can imagine my complete surprise when the announcement came from the group owners just one year after I had joined that they had agreed to sell the practice to the University of Healthcare (UHC)! The physician owners told me the reason for their decision was that all small independent groups such as ours were handing over the reigns to the large healthcare systems, and they were concerned that if they do not make this move now that our small group would be unable to compete in the changing healthcare market. I was asked if I wanted to remain with the group and become an employee of Suburban Care Associates (SCA), the clinical arm of the UHC. I was reassured that the written contract stipulated that our practice style of medicine would not change and that our schedules would remain the same. My colleagues told me they had been assured that we could continue to provide our same high quality of medical care with a strong emphasis on preventive medicine. I discussed the upcoming changes with Phil, and we decided together that I should remain with the group.

Unfortunately it was not long before we all came to realize that, contrary to what we had been told, the health system wanted high revenue at the expense of premium medical care. It was soon clear as crystal to us that there is no respect for the specialty of family medicine within the UHC and that the expectation within the system was for the family doctor to generate revenue by addressing the patients' minor ailments (quickly), and to refer patients out to specialists and to subspecialists within the health system to manage the patients' various chronic conditions. The other doctors and I argued passionately against the administrative officials at meeting after meeting against this approach; we argued that high quality medical care is deserving of increased time spent with the patients, and that we could not, in good conscience, forfeit our high standards of medical care solely to generate increased revenue. We complained to the administrative officials that it would not be in the best interests of our patients to see more and more patients each day, because this would only result in less time that we have to spend with each patient. We argued this point over and over at stressful meetings with Abigail Scruge, the frumpy Chief Operating Officer of SCA, but to no avail.

As we became busier, we voted to hire an additional doctor in order to maintain our high standard of medical care. This is the action we would have taken if we were still a small independent group. We were advised by the administrative officials this would likely result in a decrease in wages for each of us. This new doctor advised us openly she had been told that our group was considered 'slackers' by the SCA administrative officials that hired her. She said they scoffed at our schedule and she was told we would be forced to significantly increase our work load in the near future. We were extremely concerned that our employment contract, which was written to protect us from changes such as these, was being ignored. What was especially frustrating was that the medical director of SCA was himself a cardiologist. It was disconcerting to be told that we were considered to be 'slackers' by the administrative officials of SCA. If I was truly a 'slacker', then why was I both mentally and physically exhausted at the end of each work day? In our practice, it was not unusual for a patient to bring with them to their office visit a written list of five or six health concerns, and they would expect that each of these problems and questions could be addressed at their office visit, along with attention to their regular health care maintenance. We were clearly a medical bargain for our patients because we were often able to address all of their medical conditions, such as skin conditions, high blood pressure, high cholesterol, diabetes, thyroid ailments, gynecologic problems and psychiatric conditions, to name just a few conditions, during their one half hour office visit with their family doctor. Our patients appreciated the fact that we could address their numerous problems and they therefore did not have to schedule appointments with five or six different specialists. Conversely, Abigail Scruge and her business colleagues showed no interest whatsoever in our ability to provide this wonderful comprehensive and preventive health care and they instead, continued to apply pressure on us to provide quick 'in and out' medical care for our patients. We, however, could not bring ourselves to diminish the level of care that we provided, and we also knew our patients would not be receptive to such a change in their medical care either.

It was becoming increasingly obvious to us that Abigail Scruge and her administrative colleagues did not care that we work on the front line, acting on behalf of our patients, promoting wellness and prolonging lives. Our patients, on the other hand, were clearly cognizant that we have the ability to identify and treat asymptomatic conditions early in order to promote their longevity. Greed drove Abigail Scruge and her colleagues to apply the pressure to increase revenue at the expense of our excellent quality of care. I am happy to report that none of us folded under the pressure. We dug in our heels and refused to reduce our standards. Needless to say our discussions were frustrating and unpleasant each time we met with Abigail Scruge. She was never satisfied with her perceived quantity of our work no matter how we tried to explain our positions to her. Under the initial agreement, our contract was not supposed to change. As I read it now though I saw the contract had changed significantly. In effect, the ancient tradition of the caring and compassionate art of medicine had now been pummeled into the ground by the idiotic bean counter administrative officials. Our contract now read as if, instead of doctors, we sell cars, and we each are responsible to meet our quota of a specified number of car sales, alias patient visits, each year, or we will be subject to dire financial consequences. Each patient had become a faceless '0.6' (for a fifteen minute office visit) or a '1.1' (for a thirty minute office visit).

The administrative officials did not have any interest that we worked exhaustively on behalf of patients. In retrospect, the UHC purchased our successful medical practice and promised the doctors they will take care of business so that the doctors can concentrate on medical care rather than on the business aspects of medicine. This had sounded like an agreeable, logical and sensible plan. The administrative officials then turned a successful and profitable office under our management into one that was in financial dire straights under their management. They then had the audacity to pin the source for the decrease in financial success on the doctors by claiming we are slackers when, in reality, the only change that had occurred within the medical practice was the way in which the UHC conducts the administrative process!

Chapter 31 – A Broken Promise

Meanwhile, word got back to me through my patients that Dr. Harkulus continued to make it clear to his acquaintances in the area that he remained furious that he had been ousted from the family medicine office by his former partners. His acquaintances stated that Dr. Harkulus repeatedly vowed to them he would have his revenge against his former partners and he would re-acquire the medical practice. Because of this known ongoing threat from Dr. Harkulus, one of the preconditions that the group owners insisted upon before they would agree to the sale of the medical practice to the UHC, was that the health system would never entertain a sale of the medical practice to Dr. Harkulus. Kevin Spencer was the Chief Executive Officer of the SCA and he met with us frequently. Kevin would reassure everybody at our meetings that even though Dr. Harkulus kept knocking at his door and offering significant dollar amounts to buy the practice, he would never in a million years entertain his offers. Dr. Kith was especially concerned that Dr. Harkulus was hovering around trying to purchase the practice from the UHC. She would often remind Kevin Spencer at our meetings that the precondition of sale was that the medical practice would never be sold to Dr. Harkulus. Kevin would laugh and reassure us that he always tells Dr. Harkulus to go take a hike because there is no chance of a sale, ever. Despite Kevin's reassurances, we were uneasy with his reassuring words. We openly expressed concern about this promise given to us by the administrative officials at the UHC, given their back tracking on many other details that were written in our contract. Unfortunately, it turned out our concerns were well founded.

On one busy morning, our office received a call from Abigail Scruge's secretary stating that a surprise meeting was to be held at noon on that same day between the doctors and Kevin Spencer. As requested, the other doctors in the group and I congregated in the conference room at noon to meet with Mr. Spencer. For some reason, we had a sense of impending doom about what was about to unfold. Kevin Spencer was not physically present and he instead spoke to us by speaker phone. We were stunned when he sheepishly announced that the UHC had actually agreed to sell the medical practice to Dr. Harkulus! He went on to explain that the generous offer of three million dollars which Dr. Harkulus had made to buy the practice was an offer that was simply too good to refuse. I could not believe my ears. The UHC had sold the practice to Dr. Harkulus; this despite the terms of the contract dictating that this would never occur! My partners were visibly shaken and devastated. I was astonished that Dr. Harkulus had succeeded in his threats to have his sweet revenge against my colleagues. He was truly a bitter and vengeful person, one that I had purposefully chosen to avoid. I admit I was not as emotionally devastated by Kevin Spencer's announcement as my colleagues because Dr. Harkulus's deep cutting revenge was not specifically targeted at me. I did not know the specific details that had occurred before my acceptance into the practice, and I had preferred to keep it this way. Dr. Kith and Dr. Lamp however, were well aware this was Dr. Harkulus's personal vendetta directed at them, and it was clearly his successful retaliation aimed at them. After the meeting, I was saddened to witness tears fall from Dr. Kith's eyes and it was obvious she was broken hearted that her beloved practice was being taken from her in this cruel manner. She was always protective of her reputation as professional and tough, but now her sturdy spirit had been broken by the vengeful Dr. Harkulus. Dr. Kith and I had had a few spirited discussions over the years on some personal issues, but I did not derive any pleasure in witnessing this vindictive destruction of her proud domain. All in all I had come to respect and appreciate each of these physician colleagues and I genuinely cared about their wellbeing.

Additionally, I too had once again reached another crossroad in my life that necessitated another important career decision.

Chapter 32 – Solo for Them

During his devastating telephone conference call, Kevin Spencer had presented a consolation prize. The health system offered to arrange for each physician to have positions in other medical offices so that we could continue our employment with the UHC. Dr. Kith, in particular, did not trust the sincerity of the health system's offer, and understandably so, given it had blatantly broken the terms of the contract which stated that the health system would never, under any circumstances, sell the medical practice to Dr. Harkulus.

The next day, the doctors and I participated in a conference call to discuss our future options with the medical director of SCA, Dr. Coldfish. To say the call was tense and unfriendly is an understatement, and it was ending abruptly as Dr. Kith and Dr. Lamp argued heatedly with Dr. Coldfish. I certainly understood the anger of my colleagues given that the UHC had dealt us such an extraordinarily unjust hand. I still recalled my own first impression of Dr. Coldfish at an earlier time in our employment with the health system, when he instructed staff members on medical billing pearls. Dr. Coldfish was well known in the health system network as a medical billing guru and so we had positive expectations. However, after he had described his secret pearls and personal medical billing procedures, I concluded he was an arrogant and uncompassionate doctor. During the lesson, he had described to staff members his personal medical billing maneuvers and I was taken aback when it became apparent to me that he did not consider the costs his patients would incur as a result of his medical care. I realize we are in a business and that we do have to cover our expenses, but I nonetheless believe it is important for a physician to try to be reasonable with the patient's expenses that are not covered by the health insurance plan. While it is common practice for an attorney or an accountant to charge excessive amounts, I believe a physician should be held to a higher standard and the doctor should also attempt to know the personal expenses that each patient will incur because of the medical tests and procedures that are performed. Granted, this is my personal opinion, and it is one that Dr. Coldfish clearly does not share with me. Perhaps this is why he is successful working in the health system network.

During the conference call, Dr. Coldfish was unsympathetic and impatient as my colleagues expressed their dissatisfaction with the unjust treatment they had received. He then moved to end the conference call abruptly, remarking it was probably best that we part ways with the UHC because it was clear we would not be satisfied with any offer that was presented to us.

I knew that before the end of this conference call, unbeknownst to my colleagues, I would surprise everybody involved in the conference call with my own personal request. I had concluded I must part ways with my colleagues. However, this time, the underlying reason for the current mismatch was not due to a lack of fairness, as it had been at my former practice. This time the mismatch between me and my partners was political in nature. I had never discussed my own political views with my colleagues, just as I had never discussed my views on religion. I believe discussion of such personal topics can lead to heated and unpleasant discussions and they should therefore not be discussed in the work environment. Still, there was no doubt that my silence and my lack of enthusiastic agreement with many of my associates' discussions made them quite suspicious that I did not share many of their views. Unfortunately, my colleagues were quite militant and passionate in their views, to the point that if a person possessed different political viewpoints from theirs, then some unnecessary friction was created within the group. I, on the other hand, understand that individuals with all viewpoints must be tolerated and respected. I am suspicious in fact that one's political leanings may even be rooted in the individual's genetic make up. Of course, this has not been mapped on a chromosome as of this date but perhaps it will be in the future. Anyhow, as it stood, I sometimes felt like a fish out of water within my current group of colleagues. I had discussed my options with Phil during one of our evening walks around our neighborhood and he encouraged me to continue my employment with the health system and to separate from my colleagues. He and I both decided this was an appropriate time to move on. I had expressed an interest to Phil in opening my own solo practice at this time thereby becoming independent. However, after much thought and discussion, Phil and I both concluded that maintaining my employment with the health system was the best option available to me at this time.

I now spoke up during the conference call and announced to Dr. Coldfish my desire to maintain a position within the UHC. One could literally hear a pin drop because there was obvious surprise and complete silence on both sides of the conference call, both from Dr. Coldfish's phone and from my colleagues' phone. Finally, Dr. Coldfish broke the silence and advised me to contact Kevin Spencer to make arrangements to continue my employment with them. I expected my colleagues would not understand my decision and so I may experience a chilly work environment for a while. However, I also suspected my colleagues may be relieved about my separation from them so they could resume their work as their original trio of like-minded doctors. Dr. May had already announced she would be moving on from the group.

Over the next few months I was energized and excited as I prepared to become a solo physician for the first time in my career. One of my former colleagues told me that he was surprised I was not afraid to take on the challenge to become a solo practitioner. He pointed out that I would no longer have the ability to share the burden of running the practice with other colleagues. I explained to him I actually viewed this challenge to be a wonderful opportunity, because my suggestions for changes in office function and direction would not be restrained by others within the group practice who did not agree with my ideas. I told him I was surprised that he thought I would be hesitant to go forward because I was not in the least bit fearful to take on this task; on the contrary, I was eagerly looking forward to the challenge.

Kevin Spencer presented a reasonable contract to me which covered the first eighteen months of my new employment term, during which time he told me I would be busy building up a new medical office. Abigail Scruge offered positions in the new office to staff members I had personally selected. A suitable office was located and prepared to open that was situated in an affluent community called Chesterton. The first week of my work in this new office was bittersweet because it included the fateful day of September 11, 2003. I recall on that significant day when a patient arrived for her office visit, visibly upset. She explained that a plane had struck, head on, into one of the World Trade Center towers in New York. This news, in and of itself, was blood curdling enough as we envisioned the many terrified people that were trapped inside the tower, but then, as we listened intently to the radio, we were stunned to hear that a second plane had struck the other tower, also head on! Upon hearing this, we all understood this was no accident; rather, this was a deliberate, unconscionable act of terrorism.

My solo practice opened its doors claiming only about two hundred patients. My staff explained that many patients had been dissuaded from following me to Chesterton by the loyal staff of my former colleagues. Apparently, the staff members of my former colleagues convinced some of my patients to become their patients rather than sign over their records to remain under my care at Chesterton. Additionally, the sale of the practice to Dr. Harkulus was poorly organized by the UHC. Many patients unknowingly became patients of Dr. Harkulus because they had not been afforded the opportunity to release their medical records to go to the doctor of their choice. Many patients were angry when they realized their medical records were now the property of Dr. Harkulus, simply because he had purchased the medical practice from the UHC. Patients were also furious to find they had to pay a fee in order to transfer their records over to me when they never even changed their doctor! After all, they had never agreed to have their records become the property of Dr. Harkulus in the first place. Several of my patients with larger medical records told me they were charged over one hundred dollars to have their medical records released to me! Sadly, one of my elderly, frail patients got caught in the confusion. He was very stressed as he tried to switch his records and his health insurance coverage over to me so he could remain under my care. He unfortunately succumbed to congestive heart failure and he died shortly thereafter. I believe his death was a direct result of the stress he endured because of the changes in his health care. This was a sweet old man and the difficulties he experienced as he relentlessly attempted to remain under my care were very troubling and sad for me to witness. This somber experience would play a substantial role in my career actions in the not too distant future as I would be handed a pink slip by the UHC.

I was very happy at my new office even though it was difficult for patients to find initially because it was located in the back of a shopping center. I built up the practice, mostly by word of mouth from both new and established patients. Abigail Scruge would schedule meetings with me at the office on a regular basis. These meetings were becoming very unpleasant because she was adopting the same high pressure tactics that she exerted when I was in the group practice. Soon after I began operating as a solo practitioner she began to pressure me to shorten my one half hour appointments with patients down to fifteen minute visits. I told Abigail Scruge that I did not see a need to do this, especially since my schedule was not yet full. Abigail Scruge told me she was concerned patients would get used to the extra time I spend with them, and that I would not be able to crank up my speed and see more patients as the practice became busier. It was obvious to me that Abigail Scruge's interest remained solely about finances. She could not comprehend that it is important to gain a patient's trust by ensuring that their medical care was comprehensive and complete at each visit.

Chapter 33 – Dr. Stabinback

I managed the practice comfortably well on my own for the first
year, but then I received pressure from Abigail Scruge to add another
doctor since the practice continued to grow. The health system hired
Dr. Stabinback. During his interview with me he said he was leaving
his group practice in North Carolina because he wanted to be closer
to his extended family in the Northeast. Dr. Stabinback was about
my age and he was of average height and medium build. During his
interview, his answers to my questions indicated he was interested in
providing comprehensive and preventive medical care to patients,
and I concluded that we should therefore be compatible to work
together. I told Abigail Scruge I would direct the staff to schedule
some of my patients with Dr. Stabinback, if patients were agreeable
to see him instead of me, as this would help to build his patient
schedule. Abigail Scruge told me this was not only acceptable to do,
but that she actually encouraged me to do this. Even though I knew
this action on my part would negatively impact the number of
patients for which I would receive credit at the end of my contract
period, I erred and remained a trusting soul. I fully expected the
health system would take my actions to help my new colleague into
account to explain my lower numbers at the end of my contract year.
Little did I know at the time my assumption was not correct! My
mistake was to expect the healthcare system to mimic my behavior
and to behave in a decent and respectful manner. Rather, the so
called 'not for profit' healthcare system would once again mimic a
slithering, slimy snake that would throw yet another of its senior
doctors out on the street in the 'best interest of business'. Well, so
much for the healthcare system's first explanation that three million
dollars was too good of an offer to refuse. There will be no such
offer in my particular case and so a pattern becomes evident by the
healthcare system in which business needs clearly supplants patients'
best interests.

Unfortunately, it soon became apparent that Dr. Stabinback and I did
not see eye to eye on most if not all issues. Most of his responses

when I interviewed him were answers he knew I wanted to hear and they were not honest answers. Needless to say, I was most disturbed when he prescribed only two flu shots his first winter season with me, compared to the several hundred flu shots I prescribed! Dr. Stabinback had agreed with me during his interview that influenza is one of those nasty viral illnesses that can and should be prevented! I was also perturbed by Dr. Stabinback's blatant disregard for fairness. For example, in order to demonstrate fairness to Dr. Stabinback, I suggested that we share the phone call emergency medical coverage on a particular holiday by splitting the coverage into half days. I was perplexed that Dr. Stabinback was indignant and exclaimed that he needed the whole holiday off because he likes to stand around the pool table and drink beer on Thanksgiving Day. He had no concern that this might interfere with my holiday plans; his only concern was his selfish interests. I did not appreciate his arrogant manner and so I told the chauvinistic piece of pork meat that I too have plans for this holiday! When all was said and done, we did split the phone call coverage evenly on the holiday. Dr. Stabinback never demonstrated concern for being equitable and considerate toward me and so I began to respond likewise in my professional relationship with him.

The staff was frustrated and they complained to Abigail Scruge that Dr. Stabinback was leaving the office daily to go swimming or shopping and this was a problem because he was not available at these times to answer questions for the staff when his patients call with questions or problems. The staff told me they found Abigail Scruge's response to be very strange because she told them she did not expect Dr. Stabinback to sit at his desk and twiddle his thumbs during his work hours because he had nothing to do. She said that she preferred he go out and enjoy himself rather than sit at his desk and be bored. I personally think that a one hundred plus thousand dollar income each year should warrant that an employee is available to work during work hours. My own work ethic was to clean the windows, floors, and even the bathrooms when my schedule initially was not full and my staff can attest to this. I feel it is important to find work to do. This was obviously yet another area in which Abigail Scruge, Dr. Stabinback, and I differed significantly in our views.

The Chesterton staff and I were excited when a position became available in Phoenixville at one of the health system offices because a doctor had left to work in another town. Dr. Stabinback was offered the position, and we expected he would accept this excellent opportunity because he would have a full schedule of patients immediately. We were thoroughly disheartened when Dr. Stabinback surprised us all by turning down the position, saying that he preferred to stay at Chesterton. The situation was becoming tenser between me, the Chesterton staff and Dr. Stabinback because he was idle and self-serving. He would frequently attend meetings with Abigail Scruge and I fool heartedly considered these to be strategy meetings to find ways to boost his schedule.

I received notice that a meeting had been tentatively scheduled between me and Abigail Scruge because it was time for renewal and renegotiation of my contract. I knew the terms of my contract, and I was aware I would owe the health system money because, even though my schedule was full, I was not seeing as many patients in one hour as Abigail Scruge expected me to see because that would diminish the high quality of my work. I simply found the health system's expectations inappropriate and I therefore had chosen to owe money to the health system at the end of my contract period in favor of maintaining my attention to comprehensive and complete medical care. I could not, in good conscience, submit to the style of brief 'in-out' family medicine. As a family doctor, I had chosen to concentrate on making a significant difference in my patients' longevity and wellness. I preferred to sacrifice income for a good night's sleep with a clear conscience. Having said this, I remained confident that my position was secure at Chesterton because I rarely had an opening in my schedule, unlike Dr. Stabinback who rarely had a patient that was scheduled to see him! Surprisingly, although Dr. Stabinback had an extremely light schedule, he still would refuse to see one of my patients if I needed him to. An example would be in the case that there had been a scheduling error in which two patients had been scheduled to see me in the same time slot. This would be an unusual occurrence, but if one of my patients was agreeable, the staff would ask Dr. Stabinback to see the patient. It was apparent to everybody that Dr. Stabinback preferred to sit and twiddle his thumbs because he would refuse to see my patient!

Needless to say, it was clear that Dr. Stabinback and I were not working well together. Given the problematic situation, I expected Abigail Scruge was going to suggest at our meeting that I should return to my work as a solo family physician in the Chesterton office. I also expected Abigail Scruge to tell me that Dr. Stabinback would be offered a position in another office, elsewhere.

It was February 27th 2003, my husband's birthday. I drove to the administrative building of the health system to attend my meeting with Abigail Scruge. I was directed by a secretary to sit at the table in a large, empty conference room. I seated myself midway along the conference table and I then waited for Abigail Scruge to join me in the room. She entered the room a few minutes later and I was surprised that she seated herself a fair distance from me, at the end of the table. She greeted me with an awkward-appearing smile and she suddenly developed a flushed face as she spoke, "It is never easy for me to do this." She looked down at the table and spoke quickly as she continued. "Your contract is not being renewed." She handed me a long white envelope which, she told me in rushed, icy-cold details, contained information pertaining to the non-renewal of my contract with the health system. As she blabbered on with her administrative mumblings about RVU and CUV goals and objectives, and money owed by me to them, I was understandably stunned by the news and I cut her off from her ramblings and asked whose decision this was. She initially hesitated and was noncommittal in her response to me but then she claimed the decision was made by several people higher up, 'in the city'. I asked why I was losing my position and she told me it was purely a business decision and in no way did it reflect any dissatisfaction in the quality of my work. I asked if the Chesterton office would remain open and she told me it would. She then stunned me further and announced that the decision had been made to keep Dr. Stabinback employed at the Chesterton office instead of me!

I was able to maintain my composure for the entirety of the meeting with Abigail Scruge, but as I left the administrative building I was more distraught than I had been in my entire life. I wanted desperately for somebody to pinch me and awaken me from this dreadful dream, but nobody did. As I drove home, I pulled over on the side of the road despite the rush-hour traffic. My stomach was cramped up in pain and I cried in my car. This was so unfair! I had been a diligent employee of this health system for over eight years and this arrogant, lazy doctor joins me at Chesterton and in just six short months the health system is replacing me with him! I concluded this must have been the plan all along. To make matters worse, it was my husband's birthday and I had to burden him on his special day with this distressing and unexpected news when I arrived home.

Chapter 34 – Splitsville

I told Phil about my contract non-renewal and he too was caught completely off guard. I recalled that he had encouraged me to remain with the health system eighteen months earlier when all the changes were taking place due to the sale of the practice to Dr. Harkulus. At that time, I was interested in opening my own independent practice, but Phil was concerned that it would have been an enormous expense for us to bear. Phil told me he was confident that my best option was to remain employed by the health system, because I would have a guaranteed income and a secure position for the rest of my career. Truth be told, I personally never did share Phil's confidence that I would enjoy a stable and secure lifelong career with the health system. I did hope that Phil was correct and that my personal misgivings were wrong. So often, however, the health system's administration officials made it crystal clear that all clinical employees are disposable and replaceable. The administration officials didn't much care that these disposable and replaceable clinical employees included many diligent and compassionate doctors who had invested over a decade of strenuous and stressful years into their education, along with hundreds of thousands of dollars, in preparation for their dedication to their lifelong careers.

Phil and I decided it was best to shield the news of my contract non-renewal from our son, Matt, because we did not want him to worry. He was a tender ten year old at the time and we were fortunate he was an excellent student. He was in, what I describe as, 'school auto-pilot mode' and this is a testament to our early intervention to teach him the importance of good study habits. We had provided guidance to him from the very beginnings of his education in both math and reading. In addition, Matt was fortunate to be naturally bright in both literature and math skills. At this point in time, to maintain his excellent progress in school, all we had to do was to keep him on track with homework and school home projects by emphasizing their importance. He was a diligent straight A student and both Phil and I wanted to protect Matt from an excess of homework. At the same time, we wanted to ensure that Matt would benefit from the supervision Phil and I could give him to achieve academic success. We both knew the academic supervision that parents provide to their children from the very beginning of their education is crucial for their children to achieve their full capabilities in school. It is recognized that a child may perform poorly in school no matter how bright he or she is, if academic supervision is not provided by an interested parent or care-giver at home. When Matt was tested in high school to evaluate his ability in math skills, he scored greater than 99.999… We can attribute some of Matt's success in his math ability to a math study program called Kumon. Mrs. Karen Johnson, Matt's second grade math teacher, first introduced Matt to Kumon math because she used it in her regular math curriculum. Mrs. Johnson has a wonderful innate style of teaching because she individualizes her skills to the unique needs of each individual student. She told us she encouraged Matt to 'double-up' on his Kumon math assignments because he was so close to earning a medal for his excellent achievement. She told us she encourages all of her students in this manner and that some, but not all students, do increase their amount of math work so they can earn the medal. Needless to say, Matt responded well to his teacher's encouragement and he was thrilled when he was awarded a medal. But then, Matt surprised us all when he asked if he could continue to do the Kumon math program at home as well as in school. I asked Mrs. Johnson if a home program is available and she gave us the information we needed to contact the director of our local Kumon Learning Center, Laila Saidat. We signed Matt up for enrichment in math through the center and Matt progressed nicely through the program. Laila was perfect for us to work with because she allowed us to work with Matt independently. Many learning centers have an excess of rules and regulations which result in an impediment to the student's progress. Phil and I both wanted Matt to enjoy as many opportunities in life as possible. My hope was when Matt reached adulthood he will be satisfied that his Dad I planted the seeds for him to enjoy a successful, challenging and rewarding life.

Having received the devastating news of my contract non-renewal from my employer, I had difficulty eating for the next few days. My

136

gut seemed to operate in reverse peristalsis mode and my stomach literally cramped up and rejected food whenever I tried to eat. I had never experienced a situation like this in which I was unable to eat even though I was not physically ill. I knew that I was unable to eat because I was emotionally distressed in a way I had never before experienced.

I arrived at work the following morning and I struggled to hold back my tears as I informed Sally, my receptionist, that my contract was not being renewed. She was visibly shocked and she wrapped her arms around me and she cried quietly. I sat at my desk in the back room of the office before office hours began and Sally informed the staff members about my unexpected news as each employee arrived at work that morning. Each of the staff members quietly came back to me to express their disbelief and sadness that I was getting the boot and they were incredulous that Dr. Stabinback would be taking over the practice. The staff later expressed outrage to me because the unexpected decision was so clearly unfair. When Dr. Stabinback arrived at the office, I informed him of the news, even though I suspected he was already well aware of the facts, given his many 'strategy' meetings with Abigail Scruge over the past few months. Dr. Stabinback expressed surprise at my news and he told me that, now come to think of it, Abigail Scruge had made a comment at one of his meetings with her that he may be kept in place of me, although he said he never once thought for a moment that she was serious. I now assumed that his frequent meetings with Abigail Scruge were ones at which Dr. Stabinback claimed how much more efficiently he could manage the practice compared to me and Abigail Scruge must have liked what she heard from him. The staff at my office had often commented to me jokingly that Abigail Scruge appeared to have a schoolgirl-like crush on Dr. Stabinback, but I never once fathomed anything like this was going on! I take pride in that I can often anticipate what lies ahead in my life, but I have to admit that this news caught me completely off guard. It had also been evident for some time that Dr. Stabinback was not supportive of me, his fellow colleague. When employees at the other medical offices in the health system became aware of my situation, they were in disbelief. They would frequently call and joke with my office staff that the administration must be completely out of touch with reality to get rid of the busy doctor and keep the doctor that has no patients! The staff at the other offices in the health system had the ability to check our patient schedules from their computers because the patient schedules are internet based. They witnessed my full patient schedule and Dr. Stabinback's patient schedule that was essentially empty. It was laughable and the health system staff would joke with my staff about the health system's baffling decision to get rid of me and in my place retain Dr. Stabinback, the doctor with almost no patients! Of course, the health system's assumption was that the patients under my care would freely switch over to the care of Dr. Stabinback, once I am no longer available to see them. I now recalled how, from the very beginning of our relationship with the health system, Abigail Scruge would always emphasize during her discussions with me that the patients are not 'my' patients; rather they are patients of the health system. It was now evident why this was always emphasized by Abigail Scruge to be of utmost importance. It was in preparation for a situation such as this in which the health system underhandedly eliminates one doctor in favor of another without sending notification to the patients who are affected. Despite my rejection by the health system, my 'glass is half full' attitude remained untainted. I did not become bitter and I instead chose to retain my positive attitude that I can maneuver my life in a healthy and positive new direction even though I was not yet aware what it I would choose to do.

I found my work difficult over the next few days because I was confused about the news and I had not yet entered my recovery and future strategy phase. I was relieved the next week because I attended a medical conference in Florida that I had scheduled several months earlier. Attending a continuing medical education conference is an annual routine for physicians, and health systems encourage physicians to do this in order to maintain their medical knowledge. Phil and Matt would always come with me to stay at the hotel where the conference was being held. They would have some fun in the sun while I attended the medical education classes. While in Florida, I remained in a daze because I had not yet decided what I was going to do for the rest of my career. I did, however, find the trip to be a much needed break from my recent bewildering and harsh experience, and it was a welcome opportunity for me to clear my head.

138

Chapter 35 – Solo For Me

When we returned to Philadelphia, Phil and I began to consider my professional options. After a great deal of thought and consideration, we both agreed this was the optimum time to open my own solo practice. This was because I had finally completed my medical education loan payments. The most important question was location. I considered opening a medical office in my home or in my local community, close to Chestnut Hill. However, I realized it would be difficult to start over with no patients and I already enjoyed a wonderful relationship with my patients at the Chesterton office. Phil and I decided together that I would open a solo and independent medical practice in King or Prussia. We chose this location for my office because this is the vicinity of the homes of the majority of my patients, or, as Abigail Scruge would insist, the health system's patients!

Dr. Stabinback asked me about my future plans and I informed him that I might be practicing in the area and there were several options I was pursuing. Dr. Dean Drell was a Plastic Surgeon who leased an office across the hall from the Chesterton office in the medical complex and he confided in me at this time. He explained that, like me, he too had suffered an unfair ousting in the past from a healthcare system. It was apparent that he remained disturbed by this unjust treatment, and he offered me office space to lease with him because I should 'damn them all'. His disparaging comments were obviously directed at the administrative officials in the healthcare system, and I understood his angry tone and I even found his words to be comfortably supportive. His offer was certainly an appealing one since I knew those patients who chose to remain under my care would simply turn right upon entering the medical office complex instead of turning left! I advised Dr. Stabinback of Dr. Drell's kind offer to me. Just as I suspected, this news spread like wildfire, initiated by Dr. Stabinback who evidently immediately informed his health system administrative contact about Dr. Drell's thoughtful offer to me. Dr Stabinback told me Dr. Coldfish was expressing great concern with respect to my plans to open a practice directly across the hallway from Dr. Stabinback's office. It was clear to me that the health system administrative officials were paying close attention to my plans and they were now concerned my future plans could pose significant competition for their own selfish interests. I enjoyed a sense of control that the health system was well aware it no longer had me under its thumb; on the contrary, I was the one cranking up the pressure meter! I never realized that a humble doctor, such as I, could possess such clout as to actually create tension and anxiety in this prominent health system.

In addition to the offer from Dr. Drell, there were several other local doctors in the area who expressed interest and made offers for mutually beneficial medical practice arrangements. These doctors told me they knew I had a loyal patient following and they expected the patients would want to continue under my care if I remained in a local medical practice. I was greatly appreciative of my colleagues and their offers to allow me to join them in their practices or, as in Dr. Drell's case, to permit me to rent office space. Phil and I considered all my options and, when all was said and done, we still decided the time was ripe for me to open a solo physician, independent family medicine practice in King of Prussia. Another reason for this decision was to fulfill the restrictive covenant stipulation of my employment contract, which prevented me from working at an office within five miles of the Chesterton office if my employment with the health system is terminated for any reason.

I was animated and energized to move forward with my plans. I confided in the staff at the Chesterton office that I had decided to open an independent medical office. One by one, the staff members approached me to express their interest to be hired by me to work at my new office and I was gratified by their interest to continue their work with me. I expected the transition to my new office would be easier if my patients were already familiar with staff members. I therefore told each of the staff members I appreciated their interest in continuing to work with me and I offered each of them a position in my new office. I was truly delighted as each one accepted my offer of employment.

Phil and I decided that a strategic location to open my new office would be in the medical building I had worked in when I was an employee of the health system before I had moved to Chesterton. Phil stopped in at the building to speak with the building managers to ask if any office space was available. He learned there were only two spaces available in the entire building. We chose a small 1000 square foot office space on the third floor because this was the larger of the two spaces available, albeit a bit small for my needs. This space was only a shell. It had concrete floors, no partitioned rooms and the walls were not yet even covered with wallboard. The building managers allowed Phil and me to be the architects of the office. It was now almost June and we needed to have the office ready for operation by July 1st. The building managers assured us this could be accomplished. I planned to work my last and full day as a health system employee on June 30th 2003 and then swiftly transition over to my independent office on July 1st 2003. My goal was to have no interruption in the medical care of the patients who chose to follow me, other than they would be seen by me at my new office location.

Meanwhile, I continued to take care of my patients at the Chesterton office. My patients were understandably very upset that my contract was not being renewed by the health system. I recall being taken aback after I told a sweet and elderly patient during her office visit that the health system was not renewing my contract for business reasons. She was a person that considered the health system to be the absolute best and she chose only doctors within the health system to be involved in her health care. However, after I had informed her that the health system was letting me go, I was shocked because she became agitated and upset and she used profanity to express her displeasure with the health system. I was taken aback at her angry reaction because, prior to this office visit with me, she had been a consistently sweet and adorable grandmotherly-like person. I certainly did not expect her use of such profanity! I still smile to myself as I recall her astonishing response to my news. Surprisingly, she remained my patient even after I became an independent doctor and was no longer affiliated with the health system. Likewise, the majority of my patients chose to remain under my care and they articulated their distaste at the lack of dignity and respect demonstrated by my former employer to both patients and their doctors.

I was gratified and humbled by this demonstration of loyalty which had initially been expressed by staff-members, and now it was being expressed to me again, only this time by my patients. Initially, I told Dr. Stabinback of my patients' responses and he responded that he expected many of my patients would want to follow me to my new location. After a short time though, I decided not to continue to tell Dr. Stabinback of my patients' responses because one hundred percent of those I told were choosing to follow me to my new location. The obvious result of this mass following of patients to my new office would be a profound decrement in patients left for Dr. Stabinback. Naturally, I did not expect Dr. Stabinback to share in my humble bliss as it became apparent that my patients are extremely loyal and they were all expressing an interest in following me to my new office. Patients told me they were not impressed in the loyalty of the health system which would profess its concern through advertisements and on large billboards for both its patients and its employees. I never verbally discussed financial motivations of the health system with my patients but I now agreed wholeheartedly with my patients that the ulterior motive of the health system was financial, and it was not to provide the high quality healthcare that it bragged about on its billboards and on the television commercials.

My office visits with each of my patients were longer than usual because I not only addressed each of their medical issues, but I also explained to each patient why I had to leave the health system. I also fulfilled my professional responsibility to inform each patient of his or her options with respect to their medical care: They could find a new doctor, they could stay at Chesterton under the care of Dr. Stabinback, or I could continue to provide their medical care at my new independent office in King of Prussia. During the office visit I provided my patient with a record release form to sign if he or she requested to remain under my care at my new independent office. This form directed the health system to release a copy of the patient's medical records to me. At the end of each day, I added the signed record release forms to the stack of those already signed. I knew it would create a great deal of concern if the health system became

142

aware of the vast number of forms that were being signed by patients who were choosing to remain under my care. I was ensuring that each of my patients were aware of the health system's decision to terminate my contract. Additionally, and most importantly, I was not going to allow the health system to give the appearance that I had abandoned my patients, as is usually the case when a health system does not renew the contract of one of its doctors. In such a situation, after the doctor's employment is terminated, a patient typically calls to schedule an office visit with the terminated doctor and the patient is simply advised the doctor is no longer with the health system and also that the office does not know the location of the doctor. The underlying motive for this is to keep as many patients as possible within the healthcare system because the patients are considered 'property' of the healthcare system. The doctor patient relationship in this particular scenario is clearly null and void. This is all done under the radar because the health system is fully aware patients would never appreciate or accept that they are considered to be a patient of the health system and not a patient of a particular doctor.

Chapter 36 – Solicitation or Notification?

I became concerned the health system might accuse me of solicitation of patients. My contract with the health system specifically forbade me from soliciting patients. On the other hand, when patients expressed their preference to follow me to my new location, I considered it my responsibility to assist patients in the transfer to my new office, not only to avoid interruption in their medical care, but also to minimize their inconvenience as much as possible. I sought legal council from an attorney, Alan Scip, who specializes in medicolegal issues of physicians, to help me sort out this potential predicament. I expressed my point of view to Alan and he told me my actions seemed above board and reasonable, given the circumstances. He agreed that I should inform patients of my future office location and he agreed that this is appropriate notification of patients, and not solicitation of patients. To further address my situation, Alan contacted the local medical society. The representative Alan spoke with also agreed with my approach. He went a step further by stating it is not only appropriate for me to advise my patients of their options with regard to their future medical care and of my future location, but it is also a requirement of my Hippocratic Oath that I provide dutiful care to my patients. He said likewise, my employer must notify the patients of the upcoming changes in their medical care and of their options. However, he went further and said, if my employer does not inform patients of the upcoming changes in their medical care; it is then my responsibility to ensure that each patient is notified about the upcoming changes. He said my employer and I would both be guilty of abandonment of patients if the information is kept from them. He concluded that I should continue to provide patients with my best efforts to allow them ample time to make informed decisions with respect to their future health care.

Interestingly, the health system had a very different view about the situation. When Ginny Spell, the regional health system manager was advised of my actions, undoubtedly through Dr. Stabinback, she scheduled an urgent meeting with me. The meeting was held in the

Chesterton office, in a patient room which was situated next to the doctors' office. I was well aware that Dr. Stabinback would be listening in on our entire heated discussion because he was in the doctors' office at the time of the meeting. Ginny Spell spoke to me in an unpleasant manner and she proceeded to attempt to intimidate me. She warned me that the health system administrative officials had been informed I was engaging in solicitation of patients by an 'anonymous contact person' and I would be in serious legal trouble with the health system if I continued my actions. I countered her attack by explaining I was simply notifying patients about their future medical care changes and of their options, and in no way was I soliciting them. I went on to request notification by mail of the upcoming changes in medical care to each of my patients, and I also requested that patients be provided with details of the various options they have for their future medical care, given the health system does not consider it appropriate that I provide notification to my patients. I told Ginny Spell that my new office address should be included in the mailing as this will assist those patients who choose to follow me. I made my point that the health system always notifies patients in writing when a new doctor joins the health system, and therefore it stands to reason that the health system should notify patients when one of the doctors leaves their system. Ginny Spell told me that the health system does not provide mailings to patients to inform them when a doctor is leaving the health system. She offered instead to place a letter of notification in the Chesterton office waiting room four weeks before I leave in order to fulfill the health system's responsibility to notify patients about my departure. I complained to Ginny Spell that such a letter of notification would be read by a minority of patients in the practice, specifically those patients who physically enter the office within the last four weeks of my employment. By this arrangement, the majority of patients would not be informed of my removal and the goal of my employer was obviously to keep as many patients as possible uninformed and under the care of Dr. Stabinback.

When I informed my patients that the only notification the health system planned to give them that I was leaving was to place written notification in the office waiting room just four weeks prior to my departure, they were furious. My patients considered it their right to know about future changes in their medical care and they were angry the health system was attempting to withhold their notification in order to keep them from leaving. The result was that the health system's plan backfired and this only served to ensure patients would leave. Certainly, I agreed with my patients' point of view. I reassured the patients who signed medical releases to continue under my care in my independent practice that I would oversee the entire process of change in their care to the best of my ability to ensure stability during the transition of care.

Chapter 37 – The Embezzler

It was at this time that I became aware that money was being stolen from the office by Margaret, our practice manager. Margaret had joined our office about six months earlier, and up until this time I had considered her an asset to the office. At the end of each work-day, my normal routine was to review my schedule on the computer screen. I noticed quite frequently since Margaret had joined the office, a couple of patients I had seen on certain days for office visits disappeared from my computer schedule. Initially, I thought no more of this occurrence and I simply told the staff to put the names of the patients back into my schedule so there would be an official record of the patients' office visits with me. I was concerned that a health insurance company would refuse to pay for a patient's office visit if we had no official record of the visit and that this potentially could negatively impact the patient. On one particular evening, upon noticing a similar incident, I told the staff to put my patient back into my schedule as I had noticed the patient I had seen that day was no longer in my schedule. I expected to think no more of this puzzling situation but it was becoming a familiar occurrence for me. It must have been on my mind because, that night, as I was dozing off to sleep, I suddenly realized why patients were disappearing from my schedule. I concluded that Margaret was stealing my patient's cash payment at the front desk after their office visit with me. I thought this whole process through and I determined that to conceal her theft, Margaret not only removed the patient from my schedule, but she also then destroyed the 'encounter form' which provides details of the patient's office visit that the staff forward to the health system's billing office for insurance payment purposes.

I set out to confirm my suspicions when I arrived at work the next morning. I asked Sally to locate the encounter form of the patient that was missing from my schedule. It was missing. Next, I asked Sally to count the money that had been collected from patients after their office visits at the front desk the previous day. The total amount of money was appropriate based on the number of encounter forms, which were minus one. It all added up. Margaret was a thief! I was sickened as I recalled a recent event. A staff member had complained to me about an incident in which Margaret had inappropriately insisted on collecting payment from a teenage boy. She collected a five dollar co-payment from him at the front desk after his office visit with me for treatment of a respiratory illness. This young man told Margaret he only had five dollars with him and that he needed this amount of money to buy his dinner. Margaret denied his request to mail his payment to the office as soon as he arrived home and she instead took his five dollar bill despite his request to buy his dinner with the money. I confirmed this was one of the patients whose name disappeared from my schedule and that Margaret had stolen this young man's money. It was obvious Margaret could not be trusted both in the care of patients and in the handling of office money.

Later that same day I informed Dr. Stabinback that Margaret was stealing money from the office and I provided him with the sordid details of her delinquent activity. I told Dr. Stabinback we should confirm my suspicions by observing Margaret's behavior, before we report her to the administration office. I was not surprised that Dr. Stabinback disregarded my recommendation to wait and confirm Margaret's thievery, and he instead immediately reported the situation to Abigail Scruge. Shortly thereafter, Dr. Stabinback became 'Private Eye Stabinback' and he began combing through all of my patients' charts to document office visits which had been removed from the computer schedule by Margaret. The billing office in turn confirmed it had not received encounter forms pertaining to the dates of these office visits. The following week, on one evening during office hours, Margaret's administrative supervisor arrived at our office unexpectedly and unannounced. She led Margaret into one of the back rooms and clearly commenced a private and serious discussion with Margaret about the thievery. After their meeting, Margaret was instructed to submit her office keys and to gather her belongings. Margaret was then fired and escorted out of the office by her supervisor and I have not seen Margaret since that evening.

Chapter 38 – Copying Records

We were now short a staff member. The staff was overworked and it was not possible for them to copy the patients' medical records after the patients had signed a release that they wanted to remain under my care. I was concerned because it was my responsibility to ensure there was no interruption in my patients' medical care and I knew it would not be a priority item for the healthcare system to copy the patients' records to get them over to my office once I was no longer their employee. On the contrary, I was concerned the healthcare system would purposely delay the record transfer process to my office. I therefore considered it imperative that I solve this dilemma. My husband called me one day and he told me he had a solution to my problem. He suggested that we buy a copier for my new office earlier than we had planned so we can copy the patients' records ourselves at our home during our personal time. I told him this was a brilliant idea! There were about fifty or more patients each week that were signing a medical release form to continue under my care after I left the health system. My patient schedule was full up until my last day of work at Chesterton. Phil and I copied the patients' medical records at our home after office hours each day in order to keep up with the patient transfer requests. I made an extra copy of all correspondence I received from specialists about my patients and their test results if their chart was already copied and I added these papers to the copied charts. I knew it was important to keep my patients' charts current, even though this was increasingly difficult to do, especially at the point when I was trying to keep over 800 charts current! Phil was an enormous help and he was extremely supportive of my efforts. During this time my weight decreased by forty pounds and my clothes were too big. I remember buying size eight clothes that were too big for me because I still had not mentally adjusted to my new size five! I had been wearing size twelve to fourteen clothes just a few months earlier and for many years prior to this. I remember holding up a pair of size six shorts, then thinking to myself while shaking my head, "No way…" and putting them back on the rack. I went on to buy a few pairs of shorts that were about two sizes too big for me! It was a while before I was psychologically adjusted to my new small size frame and was able to pick the appropriate sized clothes! I enjoyed my new smaller size even though my weight loss was stress related, because it was closer to my pre-pregnancy weight. I have since regained the weight I had lost and I am at peace with my physical frame since I have a healthy organic sensible diet and I exercise regularly. The one thing that has changed is I have less stress and I am grateful for this.

The healthcare system sent some temporary employees to work in the office during the transition time at Chesterton because we were short a staff member. I personally gave instructions to all staff members as to what to say to patients who called to inquire about the upcoming changes at Chesterton. I told them to advise patients of their options with respect to their medical care. Specifically, I told them to advise patients that they could stay at Chesterton under the care of Dr. Stabinback, they could obtain a new doctor elsewhere, or they could remain under my care at my new office. The patients were given a form to sign for release of their medical records if they chose to leave Chesterton, and about ninety eight percent of the patients were choosing to follow me to my new office! I gave the new health system employees my business cards to hand out to patients when they asked for the address of my new office. The process was organized and it was not stressful for the employees. The health system administrative officials accused me of soliciting patients but I was not intimidated because I was confident this was appropriate patient notification. Even the new health system employees at the Chesterton office expressed no concerns with this patient notification process because they knew it was in the best interest of the patients. On the contrary, the staff would have been uncomfortable if they had to inform patients I am leaving but they do not know where I will be moving to. The staff told me this is what usually occurs in this type of situation and that they were appreciative they could provide information that was helpful to the patients. In fact I received a letter a couple of years later in the mail from my own doctor who worked for a different healthcare system which informed me she was leaving their health system. The letter withheld my doctor's future location and instead gave details of the capable care that the remaining doctors in the practice could provide. I did not want to switch to a new doctor; I wanted to remain a patient of my doctor that I had known for many years. This underscored the importance of my bold actions on behalf of my patients because I notified them of my future practice location to enable them to remain under my care, if they so chose.

My patient schedule on my last day at the Chesterton office was full up until the last possible office visit. I had finished my workday and I warmly bade farewell to the staff. As I drove away from the office I spotted Dr. Stabinback driving up towards the office. I preferred not to exchange pleasantries with Dr. Stabinback because I did not want to hide my true feelings but at the same time I did not want to be rude to him. The staff was empathetic and they clearly understood my position on the matter. I decided to continue to drive and not stop to humor Dr. Stabinback by expressing a warm goodbye as if we were good buddies. As the old saying goes, with 'friends' like Dr. Stabinback, who needs enemies?

Chapter 39 – S Denise Hoffman MD Family Medicine P.C.

The following day was a Tuesday and I was excited to open my new office in King of Prussia. The office appeared new and crisp because it was freshly painted. The color scheme was an attractive blue and white. Phil was the office IT expert and he had set up the computers, the network, and the high speed internet service. I did not plan to see patients for office visits that week unless they were sick because there was still a lot of work to be completed to prepare my new office for routine patient care. For example, the patient medical records were arranged alphabetically in piles on the floor in the hallway against the wall because we had not had sufficient time to place the charts in the file holders along the wall. I did have patients scheduled for office visits after July 1st in a book which we had used at Chesterton in the months before I left, since we had not yet selected a computerized patient schedule for use in King of Prussia. These were patients who called to schedule appointments to be seen after July 1st or those patients who had wanted to schedule their follow up appointment at my King of Prussia office after I had seen them for their last office visit at the Chesterton office. I was amazed that Dr. Stabinback seemed oblivious to these arrangements which were taking place right under his nose. This was undoubtedly because he spent so little time in the office and also because, when he was present in the building, his time was spent mostly in the back in the doctors' office and not in the front of the Chesterton office where all the activity was taking place.

In King of Prussia, I was immediately busy seeing patients who had been under my care for many years and they were excited to see me in my new office. One morning during the first week of my new office hours, a staff member was clearly alarmed as she called me to come out to the front area of the office. Dr. Stabinback had shown up unexpectedly at my office and he barged into the private administrative area as if he owned the place! I walked up in front of him and he looked over at the eight hundred plus patient charts which were now alphabetically arranged and placed neatly in the wall chart holders. "You've left me with only about thirty patients!" he complained. I wasn't sure how to respond and I replied, "The patients chose to follow me here. Many of them have been my patients for almost ten years. You said yourself the patients would want to follow me, so why is this surprising to you? I copied all of the charts myself and that was a tremendous amount of work." At this he left my office appearing very angry and distraught.

A couple of days later I had to sign for certified mail which I received from Abigail Scruge. I noticed that the letter had been written on the same day that Dr. Stabinback had stormed into my office. Dr. Stabinback had obviously visited Abigail Scruge immediately after leaving my office to inform her of his findings. The letter was curt. Abigail Scruge wrote in her document to me that I was in legal trouble because I had solicited both patients and staff to come to my new office. Additionally, she advised me she had been informed of an administrative error which had resulted in an overpayment of income to me of $50,000.00 during my last year of employment with the health system. I was well aware this was an outright lie because I had not experienced a fifty thousand dollar boost to my income at any time! Abigail Scruge suggested in her certified mail to me that I call her office to arrange a meeting with her to set up a repayment schedule. Her seedy tactics and lies astounded me! I called Alan Scip to advise him of Abigail Scruge's claims and to initiate my rebuttal of the healthcare system's claims against me. Many of my colleagues and friends had already expressed concern about my well being because they knew that the health system has deep pockets with extensive resources whereas I do not. I told them I understood my situation was similar to a David and Goliath equivalent but I was ready and eager to defend myself against this dreadful giant to prove their blatant underhandedness in court. I was in no way intimidated by their tactics and I had no intention of cowering like a spineless subordinate. I explained to Alan Scip that I value my self respect and personal courage by risking defeat much more than I value taking the easy street and simply moving on and letting things be. Alan Scip immediately put pen to paper on my behalf and he officially advised Abigail Scruge he would be representing me as my attorney to counter her unfounded and ridiculous claims against me.

My staff members and I were happy in my new independent office and the majority of my patients expressed appreciation and found my new location to be convenient to access. I was grateful to be experiencing a smooth transition to self employment and I was finding the experience much more gratifying than my former employment situation, mostly because Abigail Scruge was no longer constantly breathing down my neck, pushing me to work harder and faster, at the expense of my patients.

One morning within the first few weeks of my new location in King of Prussia, my office manager, Denise, told me of a worried mother she was speaking with on the phone. This mother and her husband remained patients of mine because they had transferred their medical care over to me from Chesterton to King of Prussia. Their son, Christopher, was a college-aged patient of Dr. Stabinback and his mother had chosen to maintain her son's medical care under that of Dr. Stabinback. She told me she thought Christopher would be more comfortable with a male doctor. Denise told me that Christopher's mother was extremely concerned at this current time because Christopher was weak due to diarrhea and vomiting. She had been unable to reach Dr. Stabinback, probably because of all the changes the Chesterton office had recently undergone. Even so, I told my staff, it is the doctor's responsibility to ensure there is no interruption in continuity of medical care, and ascertaining the emergency phone lines are operational is of utmost importance for patient care. Christopher's mother was clearly distressed about his illness and I told her she could bring her son to my office for evaluation. When Christopher arrived he appeared very ill and pale. His mother was correct; he was a very sick young man. He was so dehydrated that his systolic blood pressure was only seventy, and this, for a young male, is critically low. I called for an ambulance to take Christopher to the hospital. The ambulance crew, upon seeing a young male, told him to stand up. I was alarmed and I immediately intervened. I told the ambulance crew that Christopher is too dehydrated to stand and he will almost certainly pass out if he stands up. I instructed the ambulance crew to allow Christopher to slide over to their stretcher

154

from my office examination table so that he would not have to stand. I was not at all surprised to be informed later that day that Christopher had been admitted and he was kept in the hospital for three days because he was critically dehydrated and ill.

We have an extra person in our home. Brendan, Matt's closest friend, is two and one half years older than Matt and he actually lives with us. His family had moved from Philadelphia to live in the suburbs. They bought a house on our street and Matt first befriended Brendan when he was thirteen years old. Matt went to Brendan's house to ask if he wanted to play and this was the beginning of a close friendship. Brendan initially slept over at our house on weekends and then gradually, more sleepover days were added. The sleepovers were fine with us because the boys got along so well. Irma, Brendan's Mother, told us it was pulling at her heartstrings because Brendan missed our home whenever he returned to his own home, and he would ask constantly if he could sleepover at our house. Brendan's Father expressed great appreciation for our involvement with his son because he was beginning to perform better in school. He told us his son had found the move from Philadelphia to the suburbs to be a difficult transition but that Brendan had become more settled and self confident since we had become involved in his life. Brendan eventually asked his parents if he could actually move in to live with us. His parents gave Brendan their consent after they checked with us to be certain Phil and I would be okay with the arrangement. It was an easy change because Matt and Brendan had similar interests and mutual friends. Brendan often watched over his younger brother at our house and I was impressed with his nurturing 'older brother' skills. This was a comfortable arrangement all around, what you might call a win-win situation. Matt really enjoyed having Brendan around, and Brendan enjoyed our home and fit in very nicely with our family because he is pleasant, agreeable and easy going. Brendan's parents, in addition to their regular work, own a commercial cleaning business. They have insisted on cleaning my office on a regular basis for several years and they say it is a token of their appreciation of our friendship with them. As the years pass, this is a family we cherish more and more as time passes and our friendship deepens.

Chapter 40 – Mediate, Arbitrate or Litigate

I often spoke with Alan Scip on the phone after my office hours to discuss my ongoing legal battle with the healthcare system. Phil and I prepared many pages of detailed documents which presented my point of view and I forwarded the papers to Alan. He in turn prepared his own papers and opinions, and he discussed the situation with the attorney who represented the healthcare system. Alan raised many points on my behalf and these, of course, were in opposition to the healthcare system's point of view. It came as a surprise to me when Alan called me one day to explain he will no longer be able to represent me. He told me he had accepted a position within the UHC to work as the financial manager in a large orthopedists' office. He said he had not been satisfied in his current employment arrangement and this new position was the type of work he was ideally suited to do. I was genuinely happy for Alan. I told him he had represented me well and I harbored no resentment that his new employer would be the healthcare system that was suing me. I genuinely hoped Alan would be happy in his new position and I wished him the best for his future.

Fortunately, about six months prior to Alan's announcement that he would no longer be able to represent me, my husband had told me of Joyce Collier, another parent he had met and befriended at one of Matt's school functions. Phil told me Joyce is an attorney and he commented that she wants to hear the details about the healthcare system's case against me. She had told Phil she would like to represent me because she prefers to represent 'the little guy'. At that time, of course, Alan was representing me and I therefore had no need for a different attorney. However, things had now changed and I was in need of new representation. It was my good fortune to sit beside Joyce at a subsequent evening school function for our children and Phil introduced us to each other. Joyce has a daughter the same age as Matt and at the time the two were in some of the same classes together. I found Joyce to be warm, amicable and energetic. I asked Joyce if she would represent me in the case and, without hesitancy, she said she would. We arranged to meet at her office a few days later to initiate our work together.

Joyce and I met at her office in Plymouth Meeting and I brought along some coffee to enjoy. Joyce's office had a warm and friendly atmosphere and there were many pictures on the walls which displayed her children and some of their works of art. Joyce greeted me with an enormous smile and she invited me to sit and be comfortable. She explained that she wanted to first understand me as a person so she can represent me well, and then she will proceed to grasp the details of my case. I first gave Joyce some details about my background as she requested, and I then proceeded to explain the unexpected abrupt termination of my employment by the healthcare system, despite my deliverance of high quality medical care to my patients. Joyce expressed indignation upon hearing the facts pertaining to the healthcare system's case against me and she was unquestionably in my corner of the ring. She announced that she was eager to begin work to present my rebuttal. Joyce told me it was clear I had been treated unfairly and that I had also suffered damages because the healthcare system had not upheld their responsibility to me. I realized Joyce was correct. It was true I had expected to be an employee of the health system for several decades and it had come as a great shock to me to be terminated so unexpectedly and hideously. We together agreed I should put forth a countersuit in excess of $50,000.00. Joyce explained this would take my countersuit out of arbitration and put it, instead, directly into litigation where I would be entitled to a jury of my peers. I was confident I had behaved in the best interests of my patients and also in accordance with the law. It was therefore my preference to have a jury of my peers present to hear my case. I knew the health system had been extremely underhanded in their actions against me, especially Abigail Scruge's blatant lies of overpayment to me. I wanted the details of my case to become public knowledge because I trusted a jury of fair minded individuals would condemn the healthcare system's fraudulent behavior. My goal was also to enlighten the general public to the covert and ruthless actions of the supposed esteemed and highly respected healthcare system and its typical egotistical dealings with the vulnerable employed doctors.

Chapter 41 – Countersuit

Joyce contacted me a few days later and told me that the healthcare system still wanted my case to proceed through mediation. She said mediation would be fine if there was something to mediate. She was well aware I had no intention of accepting the opinion of a mediator who would undoubtedly seek to find a middle ground where both sides admit to some fault and make restitution. It was clear to Joyce I was confident with my case and I therefore would accept no accusation of fault. We therefore declined all requests to proceed through mediation. It was at this time that Joyce notified the healthcare system's attorney about my countersuit for an amount in excess of fifty thousand dollars. Joyce told me the healthcare system was concerned upon hearing the news of my countersuit because they were losing their control of the direction of the lawsuit. Joyce told me my countersuit would necessitate that the center city healthcare system administrative officials become aware and involved in my case and it would then become apparent that the local healthcare system administrators had bungled my situation. Joyce's eyes twinkled as she envisioned the potential scurry of alarm and activity that the news of my countersuit would create within the healthcare system.

A date was finally set for the arbitration hearing to be held in Philadelphia in December of 2004. Many of my patients wrote letters of support on my behalf but Joyce was informed by the attorney of the healthcare system that none of these letters would be accepted in court unless the patients were physically present at the arbitration hearing. Although my patients did offer to attend the hearing, I chose not to inconvenience them and I therefore declined their kind offers to travel to center city Philadelphia to demonstrate their support of me. However, one of my patients insisted he wanted to be present at the hearing to counter the claims of the healthcare system that I solicited patients to continue under my care at my independent medical office. This patient was a news producer for one of the major Philadelphia television networks, and he told me he also would bring his station's camera equipment because my case is newsworthy. My patient told me he knew the healthcare system officials would not want the details of their underhanded maneuvers when dealing with their employed defenseless physicians to become exposed to the public and available for intense scrutiny, but he said these details should be provided to the public and he was in a position to make that happen.

On Friday, December 10th 2004, Joyce came to my office to prepare Sally and Denise for the types of questions they could expect to be asked at the arbitration hearing. Sally and Denise admitted they were nervous and Joyce reassured them as best she could. Neither one had experienced anything similar to this in their past and they certainly had not expected to be called in to the court house to be questioned.

The night before the arbitration hearing, as I was driving home from work with Phil, I received a phone call from Joyce and I was stunned when she told me she had received a call from the healthcare system's attorney who informed Joyce they had concluded their claim that I solicited patients and staff from them could not be supported and they therefore had decided to claim only the issue of inadvertent overpayment of salary to me. This was unbelievable! After all the threats from the healthcare system's officials that they will have my hide for solicitation of patients and staff, the healthcare system's attorney called the very night before the arbitration hearing to advise Joyce and I it was essentially surrendering their case against me! The case was no longer a challenge because I considered the issue of salary overpayment to be a ridiculous claim by the healthcare system. Abigail Scruge was not truthful in her accusation that I was inadvertently overpaid, and Joyce and I were in possession of many documents to prove this! Since the healthcare system was no longer charging me with solicitation of patients, my patient would not be allowed to attend the hearing with the news network cameras because a counter to the solicitation charge was no longer needed. I was greatly indebted to my patient for his support and his kindness and I was actually disappointed he would not be allowed to be present at the hearing to demonstrate his support for me. Likewise, when I called my patient the night before the arbitration hearing to explain about the change in plan, he was equally disappointed. I thanked him for his support and I promised I would call him to tell him of the outcome of the arbitration hearing as soon as I was made aware of it.

That night, Phil and I arrived home from work at about eight o' clock. We greeted Matt and Brendan, and they were happy to see us as usual and we had dinner. Phil and I next changed into our exercise gear and we enjoyed our usual exercise routine designed to reduce stress and relax our muscles from the long work hours of the day. Phil, Matt and Brendan behaved no differently than usual but they knew the following day would be an important focal point in my life and one on which I hoped to prevail in my case against the mean spirited healthcare system.

Chapter 42 – D-Day

I slept surprisingly well the night before the hearing and, upon awakening, we ate breakfast then Phil and I got Matt and Brendan off to school. Some different arrangements were necessary since we had to leave earlier than usual in order to travel to center city, Philadelphia. We had no last minute catastrophes and everything progressed nicely. The boys were very accommodating even though their schedules were thrown off.

Phil and I met Denise and Sally in a coffee house parking lot in Plymouth Meeting that morning. It was a strategic location for us to meet so we could travel together in to the city of Philadelphia in one vehicle. Since we were at a coffee house we each purchased our favorite beverage before we left.

Phil drove into center city Philadelphia while I reviewed the literature which pertained to the case. We arrived at the arbitration center with time to spare. I met Joyce at the center and she was her usual pleasant and energetic self. We all entered the waiting area together. We were seated in the front row and Abigail Scruge walked straight by us, appearing stressed and miserable. Shortly thereafter, Kevin Spencer surprised me because he walked up to me smiling and shook my hand as if we were the best of friends. He said he was sorry this meeting could not be under better circumstances. I knew this lawsuit had originated with Abigail Scruge and that she had been responsible for the accusations which were brought against me. In retrospect, I wondered if Kevin Spencer's hands were tied by his executive position within the healthcare system and if this therefore was the reason he had not been as supportive of me as I had expected him to be throughout this unprecedented case.

The healthcare system's attorney arrived. He was tall with dark hair and he was surprisingly pleasant. He told us he did not expect this to take more than two hours and then it should be over. When he saw Denise and Sally were present he appeared uncomfortable and he told Joyce they would not be needed and they could leave to go shopping. My first thought upon hearing him say this was to question if he would make this suggestion to go shopping to two male employees. I sincerely doubt it! Also, it was such a wickedly cold and blustery day that they did not want to step outside unless they had to. Joyce and I agreed that Sally and Denise should stay even though it was apparent the attorney for the healthcare system preferred they leave. Joyce told the attorney Sally and Denise should remain as she probably has some questions she will need to ask them. So they stayed. I personally was very grateful for the support that Denise and Sally had demonstrated to me throughout this entire process, and I found the attorney's comments, specifically that Denise and Sally would not be needed and they could therefore go shopping, to be demeaning and offensive.

We were fortunate because my case was one of the first to be called since all individuals on both sides were present. We walked into the hearing room and Joyce and I sat together at our table while Abigail Scruge was seated with the attorney of the healthcare system. Phil, Denise and Sally were seated together at the back of the room. Also seated in the back of the room was Kevin Spencer, and he sat alone at the far end of the bench. There were three arbitrators positioned facing us and they sat at a long table in the front of the room. The lead arbitrator was seated in the middle and I estimated him to be in his late forties. On his right was a female who appeared to be in her early thirties. To his left was a middle aged male. The arbitrators appeared serious and conscientious and for that I was pleased. Before the hearing began, the healthcare system attorney announced he had to admit to a possible conflict of interest. He told us the lead arbitrator works within a company that has performed work, at times, on behalf of the healthcare system. The lead arbitrator then advised Joyce and me he would step down if we preferred but that it was his responsibility to be objective in his assessment of the details of the case and he said he was confident that he could be objective. Joyce and I both agreed he should stay because he gave us the impression he was a fair and honest individual. I personally also realized I could, as the saying goes, 'jump from the frying pan into the fire'. In other words, there was always the potential that choosing to have a different arbitrator would not guarantee a reasonable arbitrator and it could instead backfire on us.

The lead arbitrator motioned for the case to begin. The attorney for the healthcare system stood up first and he presented the facts of his side of the case to the arbitrators with great over simplification. He said the healthcare system had realized I had been overpaid by fifty thousand dollars and I had simply refused to 'come to the table to arrange my payments which were due to the health system'. He appeared to actually believe this to be the basis of the case and he did not care to consider the much greater complexities that existed. Joyce and I were frequently amused because the attorney often directed the attention of the arbitrators to his 'attractive client, Abigail Scruge'. Yes, this attorney was undoubtedly a chauvinistic smooth talker because it was evident for all to see that Abigail Scruge, through no fault of her own, was not a physically attractive individual!

After his opening statement, the attorney returned to his seat next to Abigail Scruge and it was now time for Joyce to present her facts to the arbitrators. Unlike the attorney for the healthcare system, Joyce had her facts well prepared and she was well rehearsed. Unlike Abigail Scruge, Joyce truly is attractive and slim in her professional mid-thigh length black skirt. Her voice was a little shaky as she admitted she was nervous and she requested permission from the arbitrators to stand to present her introduction. Joyce quickly gained her self-confidence and I was impressed that she spoke with great passion on my behalf as she presented my side of the facts pertaining to the case. She wrote on a chalkboard and presented details of my salary and the annual salary increases which I received as outlined in the contractual agreement by the healthcare system, over my several years of employment. Joyce then demonstrated a strikingly inconsistent sudden plummet in income by fifty thousand dollars, and she explained this would be the situation if the healthcare system was truthful in their assertion that I was overpaid by fifty thousand dollars during my last year of employment by them. By this time, because of the clarity of the figures presented and the evidence provided, it was apparent to the arbitrators that I was not overpaid in any amount by the healthcare system. Joyce concluded her opening statement by informing the arbitrators that this case had been brought against me by Abigail Scruge in an attempt to punish me unfairly. Joyce explained further that Abigail Scruge had chosen to lie in court and make false accusations against me. Joyce went on to explain to the arbitrators that this case has no merit in the claim of overpayment to me. She passionately advised the arbitrators that the false accusation of overpayment to me had been made solely because Abigail Scruge is furious that the majority of patients enrolled at the Chesterton office chose to leave the healthcare system after my employment was unfairly terminated, because they preferred to remain under my care.

The healthcare system's attorney was up next to present his facts further. He called Kevin Spencer to testify. For some reason which was unclear to me, he had Mr. Spencer present details of the typical healthcare system physician contract to the arbitrators and Mr. Spencer did so in an excruciatingly boring fashion. The discussion was so dull that I remember thinking the arbitrators would fall asleep and I was concerned I would lose the case simply because they had not been awake for most of the details. Mr. Spencer attempted to explain why the healthcare system designs physician contracts to compensate physicians in a manner similar to the car sales arena. He explained to the arbitrators the healthcare system operates on the basic assumption that all physicians are lazy. He explained further that physicians do not have adequate incentive to work hard when they become employees, and this is in sharp contrast to their willingness to work very hard when they are self-employed. To counter this potential conflict, he said the contract is designed to stimulate physicians to work harder by adding financial pressure. This entire discussion was enough to put an insomniac to sleep! It had no bearing on my case whatsoever other than to emphasize to the arbitrators that the healthcare system exerts substantial financial pressure on physicians so they will work faster and harder.

As I listened to Kevin Spencer I recalled I was disturbed several years earlier when I was initially informed the basic assumption of the healthcare system is that all employed physicians are inherently lazy. I was equally disturbed to hear Mr. Spencer reiterate this obnoxious assumption once again, only this time in court. He spoke in a matter of fact manner, as if he actually believed the arbitrators

164

would consider this, 'inherent laziness of physicians' to be a reasonable assumption by the healthcare system. I took great personal insult at this disturbing brazen assumption by the administrators of the healthcare system. I had not spent hundreds of thousands of dollars on my education, spent twelve years of my life completing pre-medical education, medical school education and then residency education, during which I worked countless thirty-six hour shifts, and also studied for hours on end, only to have these administrative nincompoops describe me and all employed physicians as inherently lazy! I wondered if the administrators of the healthcare system thought of themselves as 'inherently lazy' since they too were employees and not self employed. It would stand to reason then that they too would require a similar assumption that they are lazy in order to be productive. I suspected, however, the administrators enjoy a special status and are somehow exempt from this 'inherently lazy' assumption. I was very appreciative at this time to be self employed and no longer at the mercy of these pompous and self serving imbeciles.

I had not realized about two years earlier when Abigail Scruge informed me my contract was not being renewed that I would come to feel this way, but it was now abundantly clear the healthcare system had done me a magnificent favor by treating me so unfairly. I, for example, no longer had to tolerate the two tiered structure of employment within the UHC in which the administrators make the assumption that all employed doctors are inherently lazy while the administrative officials sit at desks within their ivory towers. I did not enter the medical profession to be treated in this unprofessional and despicable manner. In retrospect, when we first joined the UHC, I had not been involved in the negotiations because I had not been employed long enough to have become a group owner. Apparently, the UHC set the trap for my colleagues. My colleagues took the bait, and then the health system changed the terms of the contracts significantly despite the contractual agreement it will not change. The result was an unfair arrangement for both patients and physicians because it was all stacked in favor of the non physician administrators!

The questions the healthcare system attorney asked Kevin Spencer about the physician contract were irrelevant and the answers provided by Mr. Spencer were an embarrassment to the healthcare system in that it was apparent the administrators of the UHC lacked respect for their employed physicians.

Once the healthcare system attorney had finished questioning Kevin Spencer, the attorney sat down and it was now Joyce's turn to begin questioning him. Joyce directed Mr. Spencer to begin with the sordid details of the purchase of the medical practice by the healthcare system and then the healthcare system's sale of the practice to the nemesis of the group, Dr. Harkulus. If you will recall, before I joined the group, my former partners had ousted Dr. Harkulus from the group, and essentially replaced him with me. The group members confided in me during my employment interview that they had ousted Dr. Harkulus because there were several serious issues which they were not able to resolve. My patients who knew Dr. Harkulus informed me he was insisting he would have his revenge against his former partners and he would buy back King of Prussia Family Medicine.

Joyce explained to the arbitrators that the administrators of the healthcare system had sincerely promised my former partners they would never under any circumstances entertain any possibility of a sale of the practice to Dr. Harkulus, and it was only with this assurance from the healthcare system that my former partners agreed to sell their practice to them. Joyce went on to explain that the healthcare system betrayed this promise because, according to Kevin Spencer, 'the offer from Dr. Harkulus was too good to refuse'. Joyce explained further how Mr. Spencer offered to place each physician in practices in the area and that I was the only one in the group interested in continued employment with the healthcare system. She continued, the other physicians declined continued employment by the healthcare system because they had been so blatantly betrayed by it and they therefore opened their own independent practice.

Joyce proceeded to direct Kevin Spencer to describe the healthcare system medical office in Chesterton which I developed. The office was named Chesterton Family Medicine. Mr. Spencer told the arbitrators that he considered me ideally suited to the affluent practice location because of my reputation to provide high quality care. I was surprised he spoke about me with such high praise. I had expected him to indicate he had supported the decision to terminate me by claiming I was delivering substandard care to patients and that I was lazy. On the contrary, he supported Joyce's contention that I had a strong work ethic and I provided comprehensive and thorough care to my patients. Joyce was clearly frustrated by Kevin Spencer's answers to her questions and therefore she asked Mr. Spencer the inevitable, "Since you agree Dr. Hoffman is an outstanding physician, why wasn't her employment contract with the health system renewed?" Kevin Spencer looked blankly at Joyce and he replied, "I don't know. I was not involved in the decision. You will need to ask Abigail Scruge why Dr. Hoffman's contract was not renewed." Upon hearing this, Joyce indicated to the arbitrators she was finished with questions for Mr. Spencer and that she was ready to present questions to Abigail Scruge.

Kevin Spencer had received intense questions from Joyce for a full hour and he appeared weary and pale as he stepped down from the hot seat. He was not Joyce's main target because we were not certain how much of a role he had played in the unfair hand that I had been dealt. It was now crystal clear to us both that Abigail Scruge had played a major role in the unjust case against me, and Joyce was looking forward to exposing the mean spirited behavior of Abigail Scruge to the arbitrators. I was impressed at the prowess demonstrated by Joyce and that she was representing me and not the healthcare system. It was obvious she had thoroughly prepared for the case and also that she cared passionately about it.

It was apparent this was going to be a long case and one that belonged in litigation and not in arbitration. At this point, we had touched on only the tip of the iceberg, and Joyce and I both knew there were many more details to present to the arbitrators. Additionally, there was my countersuit yet to be addressed. I knew there was no possible way to complete all of the proceedings in one day, and it would not surprise me if the proceedings would take in excess of a week! Joyce, Phil and I had laboriously prepared for this case for three years and I was optimistic that my time in court would be a memorable success.

It was a surprise gesture at this point when the arbitrators asked to meet with the attorneys from both sides in private and the arbitrators motioned for the remainder of the parties to leave the room.

Chapter 43 – The Settlement

Phil, Denise, Sally and I walked out together. I was feeling exuberant because I could sense the proceedings were going well. We were happy to have a break although I was looking forward to moving on to the interrogation of Abigail Scruge. Kevin Spencer and Abigail Scruge kept their distance from us and waited in a separate room while my group stood in the hallway. I was thankful for the separation because I did not want to acknowledge Abigail Scruge in any way. As the time passed, we were becoming concerned and thought the arbitrators might be encouraging a settlement. I knew this case involved many issues and I suspected the arbitrators were becoming worried with the knowledge that this case encompassed much more than a fifty thousand dollar administrative payroll misadventure. Finally, Joyce and the healthcare system attorney walked out from the room and they stood together in the hallway and spoke to each other for a while. After a short while, Joyce came over to speak to me. She told me the lead arbitrator had calculated I could not possibly have been overpaid by the health system by fifty thousand dollars. Joyce had been asked by the healthcare system attorney if she thought I would agree to pay twenty thousand dollars to the health system. She had scoffed at the twenty thousand dollar request but responded I might agree to a ten thousand dollar settlement, at the most. Joyce was told to ask if I would agree to this amount of payment to the health system and she encouraged me to agree to the ten thousand dollar payment because she said I need to move on and concentrate on my solo practice. I was reluctant to agree to any settlement whatsoever but the pressure was mounting that I accept the offer. I reluctantly told Joyce I would cancel the countersuit but the only amount I would agree to pay was the so called physician 'production deficit' equivalent of five thousand dollars. This was the amount of money I supposedly owed the healthcare system, as ridiculous as this sounds, because I had a deficit of patient office visits during my last year of employment with them and I therefore had not quite met my 'quota' of patient office visits for the year! In other words, five thousand dollars was the amount of money I owed as a result of the deficit number of patient encounters I had which was written into the terms of my physician contract. I had a distaste to agree to any payment whatsoever to my former employer and I grumbled that even a five thousand dollar payment to the healthcare system was inherently unfair. I knew the number of my patient office visits was artificially low because the office manager had removed evidence of my patient visits from the electronic billing system as a result of her embezzlement. In addition, I had afforded my new physician colleague, Dr. Stabinback, the opportunity to see some of my patients provided my patients were agreeable, in order to help him to get established. In retrospect I was naïve in doing this but I never expected the health system and my new colleague to treat me so badly. In fact, this experience has not changed me because I continue to prefer integrity and sincerity in my associations with friends and colleagues over insincerity and selfishness.

Joyce advised their attorney I would reluctantly agree to a five thousand dollar payment to the healthcare system and I would discontinue my countersuit against it. Kevin Spencer and Abigail Scruge readily accepted my offer and the arbitrators were notified that a settlement had been reached. Before he left, Kevin Spencer wished me well and he shook my hand before he left. In contrast and true to form, a disgruntled Abigail Scruge exited the building swiftly, no doubt relieved that her ordeal was finally over.

Before I left the building I thanked the three judges for their time and interest and I shook each of their hands. One of the arbitrators smiled and he proudly told me his daughter is a resident physician at Johns Hopkins Hospital. Upon hearing this I knew he'd had particular interest in my case as such details may impact his daughter at some time in the future. Even so, we both agreed his daughter has chosen an admirable line of work, one in which I personally continue to derive a great deal of satisfaction despite having had this period of disruption that unfairly challenged my career.

Joyce, Phil, Denise and Sally were all understandably animated when I rejoined them in the hallway of the courthouse and we agreed it was celebration time. We chose to have lunch at Hoolihan's restaurant but unfortunately, our star attraction, Joyce, could not join us because she had to travel to Harrisburg to work on another case. The attorney for the healthcare system joined us in the elevator as we headed out of the arbitration center and he was smiling and amicable. Now the case was over I was congenial towards him because I no longer considered him my adversary. In retrospect, I recognized he may have helped my case considerably because he focused painstakingly on meaningless minutiae of the standard physician contract and exposed how the healthcare system demeans its employed physicians. Joyce, on the other hand, had proficiently addressed and tackled the crux of the case. She had skillfully demonstrated the many inconsistencies of the healthcare system's claims against me to the arbitrators. I am forever indebted and grateful to Joyce for proficiently maneuvering her expertise and support throughout my entire court case.

Chapter 44 – Back to Work

I was in high spirits upon returning to work and I informed my curious and concerned patients about the outcome of the case. However, for some reason, even though I was ecstatic with the outcome of the case, I wanted something more. Phil and I had invested an enormous amount of energy preparing for this important rebuttal of the lies from the healthcare system and unexpectedly it was over, after spending just two short hours in the courthouse! It was bittersweet because I was actually looking forward to exposing to the public the sordid details of corporate medicine and its disparaging treatment of employed network physicians. It was now time to let it go and move forward. Or was it? I still wanted to be a whistleblower on behalf of my colleagues who, through no fault of their own, are forced to terminate their special patient doctor bond, and also for patients who are left without their doctor with whom they have confided personal details of their lives and suddenly, without explanation, their doctor disappears. I wondered if there was still a way to accomplish this personal mission…

About a week after the arbitration hearing I received an envelope from Joyce. It contained the settlement agreement prepared by the healthcare system's attorney. Joyce added a note which directed me to first read the document and then call her. I was surprised to read the amount the healthcare system had billed me was $5,900.00 and not the $5,000.00 I had agreed to pay the healthcare system for my 'production deficit'. As I analyzed the data it was clear Abigail Scruge was responsible for the extra cost to me. I called Joyce and she told me she had already acted on my behalf to advise the administration that I had agreed to a payment of $5,000.00 and not $5,900.00, but she said Abigail Scruge refused to budge on the issue. I concluded at this point it was not worth pursuing this additional amount further and so I reluctantly wrote a check to pay the $5,900.00. It was apparent to me that Abigail Scruge is a vindictive individual and she was continuing her unscrupulous actions even beyond the settlement agreement!

I read the healthcare system's settlement agreement with a fine tooth comb before I signed it and I was delighted to discover there was no contractual restriction by signature to deny me the opportunity in the future to express my opinions about the case on paper. It so happens that I had discussed with Phil, several years earlier, my desire to write an autobiography at some future time to describe my interesting experiences as a citizen in both England and in the United States of America. I concluded my underhanded treatment as a healthcare system physician employee would serve to enrich my autobiography.

Chapter 45 – Sally

On a Monday morning in May of 2005, I arrived at work and I was informed that Sally, my receptionist, had been taken by ambulance to the hospital because she had been experiencing chest pain. She remained in the hospital for about one week and the cardiologist discharged her with instructions to continue her usual medicines and to complete a course of an antibiotic called azithromycin. It concerned me that the etiology of Sally's chest pain had not been determined at the time of her discharge. She had a high white blood count of 18,000 at the time of her admission, but the source of the chest pain and of her high white blood count remained unclear. When Sally returned to work she told me she was feeling better and I ordered some follow up blood work and a chest x-ray. Unfortunately, a few days after her discharge from hospital, Sally became increasingly short of breath with minimal activity and I actually called for an ambulance to take Sally by stretcher from my office, back to the hospital. Sally was admitted once again to the intensive care unit of the hospital for another whole week and again, I was concerned the cause of Sally's shortness of breath remained unrecognized. Sally's admission diagnosis and her discharge diagnosis was congestive heart failure. I had concerns that none of the testing Sally had undergone indicated that she had congestive heart failure. For example, upon her discharge from the hospital the second time, I obtained the blood test results from the hospital and I saw that her BNP level, or basal natriuretic peptide level, was normal. The BNP level is a test used to determine if congestive heart failure is likely and a normal level should definitely argue against this diagnosis. I called Sally at her home on the day of her discharge from hospital. She sounded discouraged and tired but she did not complain to me. I specifically asked Sally if she was any less short of breath now compared to the second time she was admitted to the hospital. Sally admitted to me she was no less short of breath. Again, I was concerned because none of this was consistent with congestive heart failure. A patient with congestive heart failure invariably is back to their normal baseline condition by the time of discharge from hospital because diuretics have been given to rid the body of excess fluid. I asked Sally if a repeat echocardiogram, or ultrasound of her heart, had been performed while she was hospitalized. She told me this test had been performed during her first hospitalization but not during her second hospitalization. Sally said she had been told during her first hospitalization that a repeat echocardiogram should be performed in the near future since a small amount of fluid was seen around her heart on the first test. I told Sally I would call her cardiologist the first thing the following morning to request an urgent echocardiogram. I explained to her it was important to confirm that her worsening shortness of breath was not caused by a progressive accumulation of fluid trapped in a closed space under the pericardium, or lining of her heart. If her shortness of breath was due to this, it would be choking Sally's heart so that it was unable to pump blood adequately around her body. This could explain that the appearance of an enlarged heart on Sally's chest X Ray on the day of her second admission to the hospital was not due to congestive heart failure, but instead, due to fluid that was trapped under the pericardium. Fortunately, I was able to arrange for her cardiologist to perform the echocardiogram the next day and he called me immediately to report that Sally's echocardiogram revealed a huge amount of fluid, called a pericardial effusion, that was life threatening. Sally was urgently readmitted to the intensive care unit a third time, to be monitored closely and to have the fluid drained from the pericardial space of her heart by an operative procedure called a pericardial window. I was thankful we now had a plausible explanation for Sally's difficulty breathing, and she returned to work shortly thereafter, breathing normally and comfortably.

Chapter 46 – They're Back!

I was distraught that winter when I had another serious unpleasant encounter with the UHC. This encounter involved billing and it was an extremely arduous and unpleasant process.

I was spending an inordinate amount of time tracking unpaid claims and therefore I hired a different billing company that bragged it was their specialty to follow up on unpaid claims. This new billing company claimed the doctor will be able to devote more time to doctoring because less time will be required for the doctor to spend on administrative duties. Unfortunately, the new billing company also proved to be incompetent. Because I routinely track all unpaid claims on a monthly basis, I promptly became aware I was not receiving any payments for my office visits from one major health insurance company. When I contacted the billing company representative to address the issue, he initially scoffed and claimed there was no problem. Shortly thereafter, during my follow up call about the serious lack of payments, the billing company representative was now equally concerned but his administrative response was pathetic. The situation became critical. It was December 23rd and the office checking account balance was critically low; I was concerned I might not be able to meet payroll! Fortunately, I kept a 'rainy day fund' that I was able to tap into for an unexpected financial emergency such as this while I desperately worked to investigate the source of problem.

The billing company was of no help to me and so I took over the reigns and I was able to identify the source of the issue. It turned out that the billing company had mistakenly billed the health insurance company in question with my old provider identification number. This number was associated with the UHC, my former employer. The health insurance company also erred because it had not updated its records with my new address and it actually mailed payments to my former employer, the UHC! We were advised that appropriate payments had been made by the health insurance company and also that all checks correctly bore the name S. Denise Hoffman M.D. However, my payments were mailed to the UHC's mailbox address instead of to my office address, and the UHC never forwarded them to me! Incredulously, the checks which bore my name had been cashed by the UHC and the health insurance company sent me the canceled checks as proof they had paid 'me' for my services. I was stunned to discover the UHC had cashed checks totaling thousands of dollars which bore my name, their former employee!

I promptly fired the incompetent billing company and hired a new company. Incidentally, I fired this third and final billing company because it also proved to be inept. I have concluded the office runs more smoothly if I manage the administrative details myself. If I identify an administrative problem, I can resolve it myself promptly. I am no longer frustrated and dependent on a delayed response by a medical billing company that promises impeccable services but then delivers a complacent attitude of 'we'll get to it later rather than sooner'.

I notified the health insurance company about the payment error and the company representative had an interesting, albeit ridiculous, suggestion to resolve the problem. He recommended I notify the UHC it had cashed checks that actually belong to me and that I should request a refund from the administrators of the UHC for the many thousands of dollars it had incompetently cashed that was actually due me. Given my history with this particular healthcare system, it was doubtful the administrators would work arduously on my behalf to correct their mistake. I insisted the health insurance company directly notify the UHC system of the payment error, and to arrange for the correction of payments to me.

To summarize this fiasco, in order to finally secure my payments I had to endure over two years of aggravation. I personally followed through on every single payment owed me. I was certain the health insurance company desperately wanted me to disappear into a deep dark hole in the ground and relinquish my claims for each office visit payment. I literally had to go to battle to obtain payment for my services. In similar fashion to the healthcare system arbitration case against me, this evolved into a matter of principle. The unfortunate health insurance representative assigned to my case, through no fault of his own, was tormented by my tenacity to acquire one hundred percent of payments which had been mailed to the UHC instead of to my office address. I suspect he may have suffered with daily excruciating persistent migraine headaches until I was satisfied the error in my account had been completely resolved. This problem had occurred due to corporate incompetence and complacency in the first place and I was therefore watchful and methodical on my own behalf to ensure corrected and accurate payments took place.

Chapter 47 – Accusation of Medical Malpractice

I have had one medical malpractice case brought against me so far in my career and I hope it will be my last one! The situation arose six years after I entered independent solo practice and I remember it well. I received certified mail advising me I was being sued for medical malpractice by the family of a patient I had seen only one time; I had sent her to the emergency department from my office and she died several days later. I immediately wrote a narrative about the case to ensure I would remember the major details of the medical care I provided to this twenty five year old female patient from India while it remained clear in my head. I knew many malpractice cases do not come to trial for several years and I wanted to be certain to retain all the important details involved in my care of this unfortunate patient before she died.

I was annoyed when the initial attorney that was assigned to represent me was disturbed that I had written this narrative without his recommendation. I sensed he had a pompous and condescending attitude toward me when we spoke on the phone about the lawsuit, and on one occasion my husband overheard one of the phone discussions I had with him. After I hung up the phone, my husband asked me whose side the attorney is on! It was apparent I needed a different attorney even though I was informed by David, the representative for my medical malpractice insurance company, that this attorney is the best in Philadelphia. I advised David I want an attorney that respects my independent attitude and also one that recognizes attorney and doctor will have the most success if they respect one another and work together as a team. David told me his company was concerned that I was not satisfied and he promptly located a different attorney for me. Michael McGilvery replaced my former attorney and he immediately came to my office to meet with me. His approach was already superior to the attorney I had fired because the former attorney had never bothered to meet face to face with me. I immediately sensed Michael's style was more relaxed and professional as he set about getting to understand the details of the malpractice case which had been brought against me. He was seasoned, respectful and had a relaxed, pleasant personality. I presented my narrative to him and I have included it in this chapter. He told me he appreciated my strategy and that the narrative was an invaluable tool refresh my memory periodically over the next few years before the case comes to trial.

Narrative written September 2012:

In September 2012, a twenty five year old Indian female presented to my office as a new patient with complaints of fever, sore throat, swollen lymph nodes, and rash. The patient had agreed to an initial evaluation by a nurse practitioner student who, in turn, reported her assessment of the new patient to me. The student and I then evaluated the patient in her room, together.

The patient stated she had recently moved from North Carolina to Pennsylvania to be with her fiancé. She had a history of polycystic ovary syndrome which was treated with a medicine called Aldactone. She had developed an acne infection on her right cheek and Bactrim DS, a sulfa medicine, had been prescribed for this. A few weeks later, the patient had developed a fever, sore throat, rash, swollen lymph nodes, and fatigue. A rapid strep test was performed by my medical assistant to test for strep throat and it was negative. The patient had an elevated temperature of 102.6 degrees F and her blood pressure was 100/70. She had an increased heart rate due to her fever. Her throat was red and she had tender neck and right axillary lymph nodes. I explained to my student that under normal circumstances I could treat a patient such as this myself and observe her closely over the next several days to confirm improvement. However, in this patient's case it was most prudent to send her to the emergency department for further evaluation and management because the possible etiologies of her illness were too complex to be confirmed without further testing. I explained to the patient and her fiancé it was necessary to send her to the emergency department and I made arrangements for the emergency department to anticipate her arrival. I communicated to the emergency department my concerns;

this is a young patient with a high fever, a negative rapid strep test, a rash, and a possible sulfa drug reaction, among other possibilities.

After the patient left my office, I took the opportunity to teach the nurse practitioner student an important lesson. The patient had explained that her family friend who is a physician and had met this patient only one time recently at a family function, had instructed her to take two Bactrim DS (sulfa) tablets daily instead of one when she had developed her fever and sore throat. I stressed to my student that Bactrim should never be used to treat possible strep throat infections as it is not effective for this condition. It is stated as such in the Bactrim professional literature itself. Also, I stressed a doctor should not increase the dose of an antibiotic when a fever has occurred while on that antibiotic because the antibiotic may simply not be effective or because the patient's symptoms could be solely due to Bactrim! Drug fever due to Bactrim is a well known entity and this is why it is not recommended for long term use such as for treatment of acne. I explained to my student that the patient's medical family friend should have instructed her to stop the Bactrim immediately and to go to an emergency department for evaluation of her symptoms. Unfortunately, her family friend did not follow these simple steps and therefore the patient did not present to me until four days after her initial symptoms had developed.

In effect, the patient was a victim of medical negligence by her own family friend:
- Her symptoms could have been due to drug fever caused by Bactrim DS and doubling the dose was the worst possible action to take.
- Bactrim DS should never be prescribed to treat strep throat, and this was one of the possible etiologies of her illness.
- A change in treatment was clearly indicated and not a continuation of treatment since a fever occurred on the treatment.
- Bactrim DS is not indicated for treatment of acne lesions because of its well known association with drug fevers and potential death.

- Bactrim DS should not be prescribed with diuretics due to potential interactions. This patient was taking Aldactone for polycystic ovary syndrome.

It is my normal routine to follow patients though to wellness after I have seen them in my office, and so when I arrived at my office the following morning on 09/11/2012, I asked my office manager to contact the patient for an update with respect to her medical condition and also to call the hospital to obtain the patient's emergency department record. When we did finally reach the patient at about 2pm that day, she advised my office employee she had been diagnosed with Mononucleosis and had also been instructed to stop the Bactrim. I was busy evaluating my scheduled patients while at the same time communicating with the patient through my office manager at my front desk. I was advised of her condition and I was very concerned because her condition was worse. She reported that her temperature was 103 degrees F, her throat was still sore, she described flu like symptoms and now she reported low back pain and blood in her urine.

I told my office manager to advise the patient she must return to the emergency department because I did not agree the diagnosis was Mononucleosis. She refused to return to the emergency department because she said she had just been there. I then asked the patient to permit me to schedule an urgent appointment with an Ear, Nose and Throat (ENT) specialist. This would be my alternative means to get the patient the appropriate medical attention she needed. I expected the specialist would correctly rule out Mononucleosis as a diagnosis and send the patient back to the emergency department to get the urgent medical attention she needed. I was perplexed because she refused to return to the emergency department, and she also would not allow me to arrange an urgent evaluation that same day by the ENT specialist. It was highly unusual for a seriously ill patient such as this to disregard instructions from her doctor. I concluded she must lack confidence in my medical judgment because I had seen her only one time. I continued to insist that she must return to the emergency department for re-evaluation, but she never did heed my crucial and probably life saving advice.

The patient scheduled an appointment to see me in my office two days after her emergency department evaluation as this had been recommended by the emergency department doctor. I was relieved when she called on the day of her appointment on 09/12/2012 at 9am to cancel her office visit with me and to report she was returning to the emergency department instead. That evening, after I had completed my office patient appointments and before I left my office, I called to speak with the patient to inquire about her second emergency department evaluation because I had not received any reports from the hospital. I was told by her fiancé that she was sleeping. He told me she had improved a lot that day and therefore she had not gone to the emergency department after all. I was pleased with his report of her recovery but I explained even though she was improved she did have some mild lab abnormalities that needed to be rechecked. I recommended that they stop by my office the following morning to pick up a requisition to get some follow up blood tests. Although I was relieved she was finally improved, I also ordered a test for confirmation of Mononucleosis because I remained highly skeptical of this diagnosis.

I was stunned when I received an urgent phone call from a hospital representative upon arriving at my office the following morning on 09/13/2012, to advise me of grave news. I was informed that the patient's fiancé had rushed her to the emergency department in the middle of the night because she was crying out in agony due to severe abdominal pain. Upon arrival at the hospital, she was determined to be critically ill and she died shortly thereafter on the operating table, despite desperate emergency efforts to save her life.

A few days later, the patient's father contacted me by e-mail and I corresponded with him about his daughter's unexpected demise and I sought to console him. I also spoke by phone with additional family members who are doctors both in this country and in India. A particular family member criticized my medical care but then she backed off when I retaliated and asked how her actions would have been different from mine. I was comfortable communicating with the patient's family because I knew I had done everything within my power to get her the help that she desperately needed. My staff was astonished to learn I was being sued because they knew how much we had all tried to assist the patient to get the appropriate follow up care she needed. I do think there were other factors involved that kept her from following my directions and treating me as her primary doctor. Based upon the patient's prior receipt of medical advice from her family medical friend, I suspected the patient continued to receive advice from this person who most likely agreed with the emergency department diagnosis of Mononucleosis. This was the only explanation I could fathom as to why the patient did not follow my instructions and return to the emergency department when she failed to improve. This was a very frustrating situation for me and my office staff and it resulted in a tragic outcome.

By April 2014, I had been provided copies of the fiancé's deposition and I also had the opportunity to read all of the patient's text messages. It was apparent by her text messages to her fiancé that she would have followed my instructions and returned to the emergency department, but her relatives told her this was not necessary because the Mononucleosis will resolve on its own by two weeks. The patient's fiancé states in his deposition that her aunt who is a doctor in India, corresponded with her niece by phone and told her the blood in the urine was due to 'vaginal tears' and was of minimal concern. The fiancé also reported that the aunt reassured her niece through text messages that she would be fine and to drink water that contains some glucose and some electrolytes!

It was apparent by reading the fiancé's deposition that my recommendations were undermined by the patient's aunt, the patient's family friend that is a doctor, and by other family members who are also doctors. These individuals all behaved as though they knew better than I did, even though I was the one who had actually examined the patient.

It was also apparent in the fiancé's deposition that he was particularly busy at work that week and he unfortunately put greater emphasis on his work than on his fiancé's wellbeing. I believe this fact also contributed to her death.

In conclusion, after careful study of all the facts in this case, it is my opinion that the patient would be alive today if her family members, and also the friend of her family, had not texted in agreement that 'Dr. Hoffman is hysterical' and they instead chose to obstruct my medical care. The fiancé also bears significant responsibility because he did not take her back to the emergency department even though he read her text message that read 'Dr. Hoffman insists I return to the emergency department for re-evaluation and treatment'.

Many hours of preparation were associated with this case over the next three years both by me and my husband, and my attorney. I endured the interrogation by the plaintiff's lead attorney who I shall appropriately name 'Pit-bull'. My deposition lasted twelve grueling hours and on these days I was not available to provide for the medical care of my patients. My colleague, Dr. Lucy Hornstein, has a medical office close to mine, and she was very gracious and provided coverage for my patients while I was not available to them, because of my involvement associated with the case.

My deposition was long and tedious. Pit-bull was nasty and smug. She badgered me with the same questions again and again and she repeatedly insulted me inappropriately. At several points, Mike McGilvery expressed frustration because Pit-bull was merciless toward me, as she desperately sought inconsistencies in my deposition. However, there were no inconsistencies, much to Pit-bull's dismay, because I was sincere and truthful in my responses to her questions even though it was obvious Pit-bull was attempting to fluster and intimidate me. At one point I seized the opportunity to counter her accusations. I was aware that Mike had copies of the patient's text messages in his briefcase and I was also aware that all depositions are recorded. I exclaimed to Pit-bull, "Why are you lying? Why do you repeat over and over that I did not tell the patient to go to the emergency department when her own text messages to her fiancé confirm I insisted she should return to the emergency department?" Pit-bull appeared stunned by my offensive tactic and Mike confirmed to all present that he had copies of the text messages in his brief case. He scrambled to retrieve the patient's highlighted text messages from his brief case and he handed them to Pit-bull to read. Pit-bull appeared concerned and uneasy as she looked at the papers before her. This proved her to be untruthful while being videotaped in the presence of many attorneys. Turnabout was fair play, I had decided, especially when I had evidence in the patient's own texted notes to confirm my honesty and to expose Pit-bull's deception!

I was most unhappy to discover this portion of my deposition had been redacted and it was not included in the copy I received. I e-mailed Mike to request a copy of my original deposition and not a redacted version, but much to my displeasure, it was never provided to me. I concluded the requirement 'under oath' pertained only to me, the defendant, and not to Pit-bull, the plaintiff's attorney. I suspect this portion of my deposition was an embarrassment to Pit-bull and it was deleted at Pit-bull's request by those that have the authority to do this. I was allowed no say in the matter, other than to have the satisfaction of documenting that it happened, here in my book, now.

Members of my staff that had interacted with the patient in any way were similarly harassed by Pit-bull during their depositions. Each of them described a harrowing experience. Their experiences were similar to mine; Pit-bull approached them as if they were actual criminals and demeaned their characters repeatedly. They were incredulous they had to endure Pit-bull's attempts at character assassination when they had only had the patient's well being in mind. The patient's family had chosen a ruthless law firm with a reputation for turning a blind eye to truth and justice in their mission to attempt to win a multimillion dollar settlement for their client.

Mike and a colleague of his, Denise Juliani, continued to work diligently on my behalf. They kept me informed and met with me regularly to update me on the case. Mike located several highly reputable expert witnesses from prestigious academic institutions to represent me and it was apparent they had studied the case thoroughly before they wrote their detailed, highly supportive reports about my medical care. Phil and I were provided with all of the patient's pertinent text messages and also the dates and times of phone calls the patient made to her fiancé, her family and to all medical facilities. Phil and I used this data to document and therefore provide evidence of the exact time sequence of the patient's actions, and this served invaluable to prove that my testimony was

186

always truthful. Additionally, this time sequence of events exposed Pit-bull's accusations of my negligence as outright lies!

D Day finally arrived! I had been told to expect to be in court for 2 to 3 weeks. I was thankful to Dr. Hornstein because she provided medical coverage for my patients during this time. I met with Mike each morning in the cafeteria at the courthouse before the proceedings to discuss relevant facts of the case and appropriate strategies. We were pleasantly surprised that a junior attorney with the firm would be trying the case and not Pit-bull. Mike told me it appeared the law firm was not expecting to prevail in this case and therefore a junior Pit-bull was their sacrificial lamb. I was surprised I had not been dropped from the case by the plaintiffs' attorneys because I knew I could prove that the patient's family worked against me, and that they were the ones actually guilty of medical malpractice. I was going to prove that I had tried desperately to get the patient the appropriate medical care she urgently needed and Mike, Denise, my husband, and I had worked meticulously together to demonstrate this. The other defendants named in this case were an emergency department physician, an anesthesiologist, and the hospital.

Juror questioning and selection was very interesting. I was pleasantly surprised how many of the jurors had experience in one way or another with the perils of a sulfa allergy because I knew the lawsuit was going to focus on this. The judge was pleasant and he made a conscientious effort to relax the atmosphere in the courtroom. Mike told me this judge has a reputation that precedes him and that he is usually strict but fair.

During the court case I had to endure many terrible accusations and lies about my office staff and about the care I provided to the patient. At one point Pit-bull must have sensed things were not going well for the plaintiff because she presented a bizarre verbal complaint to the judge that I was 'laughing exuberantly' with a colleague outside the courtroom. This was a ridiculous accusation because I had no clue at the time what the outcome of this case would be. The judge was professional and addressed Pit-bull's accusation seriously before determining it had no merit. Incredulously, a short time later, Pit-bull presented yet another verbal complaint about me to the judge. She whined to the judge that I spoke to another defendant about the case in the presence of one of the jurors while we were in an elevator together. Again, the judge was very experienced and proficient in his response. He asked Pit-bull to identify the juror that was present in the elevator during our supposed 'discussion' and he called this juror into the courtroom while the other jurors waited outside. He asked the juror if I had discussed the case in the elevator with another defendant in his presence. The juror confirmed there was no truth to Pit-bull's accusation and that was that, we were told by the judge we must move on. I concluded Pit-bull was behaving in a very strange non-objective manner and that perhaps she was close to having a full blown mental breakdown.

It was a difficult two weeks because at the end of each day I spent several hours at my office to check on patients' test results. My staff and Dr. Hornstein did an admirable job to reduce my work load as much as possible but there still remained hours of paperwork to review. I had never given much thought to the huge piles of paperwork I comb through each day; I simply always kept up and accomplished the important task because my patients deserve to have the best medical supervision of their care that I can possibly provide. I will always consider it a great privilege to earn the confidence and respect of my patients.

When the time came for Mike to deliver his closing statement I was astounded by his prowess. He told me immediately after that he was anxious and had been sweating profusely under his suit! I had never realized how nerve racking it is for attorneys to represent their clients. Mike confided during the two weeks of my court case that he experienced daily angst and difficulty sleeping. I conclude the attorneys present themselves well and I have the utmost respect for those that represent innocent doctors against fraudulent claims. Mike zig zagged effortlessly throughout his closing statement, and he adhered meticulously to the precise timeline of phone calls between the patient and her family, text messages and chart documentations. This provided the jury with absolute proof of the patient's actions at the time of my care. Mike demonstrated he knew this case like the back of his hand and he appeared to have a photographic memory as he detailed crucial intricacies about the case. At the end of his closing statement, he told the jury he had been very proud to represent me and that, in conclusion, I was the only professional involved in the patient's medical care that was correct about her diagnosis from beginning to end. Actual patient tissue slides had been forwarded to the Center for Disease Control of America and it was concluded that the patient had died due to a drug reaction. As Mike said in his closing statement to the jurors, "Dr. Hoffman was right from beginning to end!"

It was time for the final verdict. The jurors convened for approximately 2 hours and my supportive husband waited with me in a local café until we were called back to the courtroom. This was it, this was the moment! The lead juror read the verdict aloud: The jurors find Dr. Hoffman zero percent negligent. The jurors find the plaintiffs one hundred percent negligent. I was exuberant with the verdict but I remained quiet as the additional verdicts for the anesthesiologist, the emergency department doctor and the hospital were read. The jurors decided some negligence existed on the part of the anesthesiologist regarding a potential medication dosing error in the operating room, but they concluded this had no bearing on the final outcome of the case because the patient was so critically ill by the time she arrived at the hospital. Additional remaining verdicts were zero percent negligence for both the emergency department doctor and the hospital. The plaintiff received no monetary award at all. Justice did prevail! It was a relief to have this nightmare over and done with and I was ecstatic to have demonstrated that negligence did exist, but it was on the part of the patient's family and not in any way due to my actions! I made many phone calls that evening to concerned family members who had been disturbed that I had to endure this unfair ordeal in the first place. My family members were all relieved to hear the final outcome of the case. My representative from the medical malpractice insurance company later told me a verdict of 100% negligence on the part of the plaintiff is virtually unheard of. I concluded that great outcomes can be achieved through great teamwork! On our way home that evening, Phil and I stopped at Mike's office to deliver a well deserved and appropriate case of beer made by the Victory Brewing Company!

Chapter 48 – Present Day

My work is currently two-tiered. First and foremost I take care of
my patients clinically. Secondly, I also supervise the administrative
aspects of the business. The first tier of my work is the most
rewarding and enjoyable aspect of my career. I thoroughly enjoy the
interaction I have with my patients and I work hard to keep them as
healthy as I possibly can. I was profoundly grateful when my
patients that, according to Abigail Scruge, 'belonged to the UHC'
chose to remain under my care at my independent medical office and
not within the well known UHC system. I suspect the scorned
Abigail Scruge would ask to this day, why patients would leave a
reputable and famous healthcare system and choose to remain under
the care of a no name family doctor, such as Dr. Hoffman. The
answer is simple but it is important; patients are not items to be
owned. Their loyalty should never be taken for granted. The subject
matter discussed behind the closed doors during an office visit
between the doctor and patient must always have the potential to be
confidential, if the patient so chooses. There is no visit more
gratifying to me than a patient who is new to me that is initially
anxious, but then leaves my office relieved and relaxed because I
have addressed all of his or her health concerns in a non-threatening
professional and friendly manner.

Patients frequently tell me that they want to be able to choose their
own doctor, and many new patients have complained they were
scheduled with a different 'provider' for every encounter at their
prior medical facility and this was the reason they changed to a new
medical office. Many patients inform me they actually seek out an
office which has only one doctor available to see patients because, at
their prior office, they had been scheduled to see a different doctor at
every single office visit and they grew frustrated at the resulting lack
of continuity of care. Many patients themselves want to cultivate the
doctor patient relationship. Patients know this special relationship in
a primary care office forms the basis for preventive medicine and it
also provides for their long term well being. In ideal circumstances
the patient has the utmost respect for his or her doctor and likewise,

the doctor has the utmost respect for his or her patient of many years and sometimes, many decades!

Made in the USA
Middletown, DE
10 July 2018